FOREWORD

When we talk about recommendations, introductions and networks, it is easy to overcomplicate. They are all part of your personal brand, of course, but what really matters is a personal connection based on your mission and values.

Here at the thePower, we are about democratising knowledge. When I followed a lead and sat down with the co-founder of a tech unicorn, he looked me in the eye and felt we could do business together. The personal still matters: the promises you keep and the trust you inspire.

From such beginnings, we grew like a rocket. Then, after four years, we had to rethink everything, as Covid changed the way everyone felt about themselves when they realised that life was shorter than they thought. We had built our network of 300 associate professors through recommendation and we have kept them with us. Even if we have broadened what we now offer to our 200,000 students, our mission remains the same.

That's why I am so happy to welcome Robert Flint's book. In the modern workplace, it's easy to think you can take shortcuts. Let digital carry the load. Of course, systems matter, but growth still relies on your ability to collaborate and network, to partner and share. It's not the number of interactions that matter, but their quality. At thePower, we now have a whole team building up these connections.

Some of us are naturals, fortunate in how we grew up. The rest of us can learn more about how to establish trust when working with strangers. What is certainly true, particularly in an environment as demanding as the modern workplace, is that we can all improve.

It's why Robert's book is such a valuable addition to our knowledge of how to grow in business and in life. Instinctively, you will recognise he is pointing you in the right direction. Even so, it might require decisions that are not easy to make. If, like us at thePower, you have a strong sense of mission and an ambition to grow, then it will be highly rewarding for you to follow what Robert has to say about how far a modern referral strategy can take you.

**Rafael Gozalo, co-founder and
co-chief executive, thePower**

INTRODUCTION

The ability to work with strangers on complex problems makes humanity unique. We collaborate across vast distances and extended networks with people we barely know. It makes us greater than the sum of our parts and allows the global economy to function. Collaboration is our superpower.

We all instinctively know what it means to collaborate: working in a team, sharing knowledge, ideas and resources to achieve a goal. It requires trust that your teammates are competent and will keep their word. Without collaboration, we would still be driving our prey over cliffs and lighting fires with a flint. The first archaeological evidence of civilisation, the celebrated anthropologist Margaret Mead is supposed to have said, is a healed human femur. Other animals with a broken thigh bone die slow deaths. Humans collaborate and live.

This book is called *Working with Strangers* because that is how collaboration in the modern economy starts: the aim is to stop being strangers as quickly as possible. The process of collaboration itself is one of the best ways to come to know, like and trust each other.

While we may understand collaboration, no one teaches us how to make referrals, which are the principal characters in this story. It is assumed that we know what they are and how to make them. It is assumed that they are easy.

Historically, referrals have relied on the old boys' network, copious alcohol and interminable golf. At its worst, this process is exclusionary and corrupt. Think mates' rates, backhanders, greased palms and mutually scratched backs. The English language has plenty of phrases for the sinister side of referrals. In the modern world we can do better than this, and not just because those historic informal networks are dominated by elites.

Many service businesses grow by referrals, from sole traders to the Big Four professional services firms. But we service providers are all amateurs at making successful referrals. That's a problem: getting it wrong costs time, money and, if it goes wrong, our reputation too. We are leaving value on the table and missing out on great growth opportunities that don't cost the earth. Referrals don't just help us grow our revenue, they help us thrive sustainably.

As a corporate lawyer who runs Adviserly, the global referral network of boutique law firms, the business benefits of referrals are clear. Organic referrals are the best source of work for most of our members and, if you're reading this book, that's probably true for you too. But we're not taught how to make or receive referrals.

A modern referral strategy is as important for a business as a marketing plan and as vital for an individual as a career development plan. It is the easiest way to build a client base and grow your business. And you don't need any additional expertise or a big budget. Improve what you are already doing and systematically repeat it. *Working with Strangers* helps you put together the strategy to make your career and business thrive.

WORKING
WITH
STRANGERS

BUILD YOUR CAREER AND
GROW YOUR BUSINESS
THROUGH REFERRALS

Working with Strangers: Build your career and grow your business through referrals

Every possible effort has been made to ensure that the information contained in this publication is accurate at the time of going to press. Neither the publisher nor the author can accept responsibility for any errors or omissions, however caused. Nor can any responsibility be accepted for loss or damage as a result of reading this publication.

Published by Novaro Publishing Ltd, 2 Speedwell Drive, Lindfield, West Sussex, UK
e: publish@novaropublishing.com.

© Robert Flint

The right of Robert Flint to be identified as the author of this publication has been asserted by him in accordance with the Copyright, Design and Patents Act 1988.

ISBN: 978-1-7398640-9-5

A CIP catalogue record for this book is available from the British Library.

Designed by Chantel Barnett, Clear Design CC Ltd

For further details about our titles and our authors, see:
www.novaropublishing.com

WORKING WITH STRANGERS

BUILD YOUR CAREER AND GROW YOUR BUSINESS THROUGH REFERRALS

ROBERT FLINT

For Dad and his first rule of working with strangers: be polite

CONTENTS

Appendices

What is a referral?

A referral is one of those words that sits in the background of language without taking centre stage. There are no poems or hymns to referrals. No plotlines hinge on a whether a referral is made in the nick of time. It's hard to imagine the word forming the punchline of a joke, even a joke about referrals. It's just not a prepossessing word. We think it's time that changed.

Let's start by figuring out what we mean by a referral. At its broadest, a referral is a type of collaboration in a work context. We define a referral like this:

$$Referral = recommendation + introduction$$

The recommendation is the key part here because of what it represents. The person making a recommendation puts their reputation on the line. For service businesses, reputation is vital for receiving future work and maintaining a personal brand. In some cases, making a recommendation involves regulatory or insurance risk. Recommendations should not be made lightly.

A recommendation is powerful because of what it does for the client. For many, instructing a professional adviser or tradesperson is a daunting prospect. People come to divorce lawyers when they are in stressful situations and need help. They come to builders when they want to extend their house. Everyone knows a horror story of a bad lawyer or a bad builder. The stakes are high.

Clients face too many options and are usually not well equipped to choose between them. They don't know what good looks like. After a while, every accountant's website looks the same. There are many variables when choosing a professional, including quality of advice, value and responsiveness to name the top three. Non-experts don't know how to compare one to another or decide who provides the best value. The client is always at risk of being ripped off and they know it.

A recommendation from someone a client trusts is powerful because it responds to that jeopardy and narrows the choice. It reassures them that they are not alone: someone like them has been on this road before and knows the way. Clients who come to you from a recommendation already trust you to help them achieve their goals, because they trust the person who referred them to you.

The person making the referral has hopefully picked you because you are good, and because you match what the client is looking for, both in terms of quality and personality. It follows that clients received through referrals are more likely to know and appreciate what you do, pay your fees on time, and stick with you.

Compare these referred clients to those who come to you without a recommendation: typically through organic traffic to your website or paid advertising. They will know you have a nice website that ranks highly in search results, but they know little else about you. They may be suspicious that they have been suckered by clever marketing, and alert for evidence that they have made a mistake. Without a recommendation, they may not value you as highly or fully understand what it is that you do.

The second part of the equation, the introduction, is more straightforward. It is a simple act such as sending an email or bringing people together at a party. An introduction is not in itself a referral, which requires some form of recommendation beyond saying that two contacts have a lot in common. If you are introducing two people you have just met to each other, you are not making a referral. An introduction is a link in a chain between individuals.

The more introductions are made within a community between different people, the more those links look like a web of relationships holding the community together. Zoom out from one introduction between two people and look at the many introductions within a community and we see that an introduction is the essence of collaboration.

Referrals are often more complicated than this. They include an extra element of teamwork or project management. It is common for service providers to refer a client to other professionals with different expertise and then work with them as a team. The equation for these complex referrals looks like this:

Complex referral = recommendation + introduction + teamwork

We can see the potential for big projects to arise within complex referrals. Imagine a community of freelancers that frequently works together on client projects. Individually, they only service a few clients within their area of expertise. Together, they service larger clients across multiple skillsets. The same applies to larger service providers like marketing agencies: in essence, just professionals working in teams and making referrals between each other in a systematic way. Whether you are furthering your career in a big firm or growing your small business, complex referrals and collaboration are the essence of what you do.

Both simple and complex referrals are hard: they are personal, so they reflect our human flaws. We don't know each other as well as we think we do. We struggle to judge if a service provider who is right for one client is right for another. Referrals are old fashioned and not terribly efficient. They can reinforce existing power networks. You never know when referrals will find you and they are hard to measure. They feel too irregular to form the basis of a thriving business.

Yet what referrals lack in efficiency, they add in resilience. Even if your other lead generation processes fall away, referrals will continue. When your business goes through a tough patch, it is your friends and partners in business who will help pull you through. Human involvement in making a recommendation is better than an algorithm, at least for now. Business consultants talk about efficiency. But for businesses it is resilience, staying in the game, that matters. Like our ancestors, it is how we fix the broken thigh bone.

Referrals are a great way to grow your business because you can:

- make money through inbound referrals;

- offer a wider service to clients through outbound referrals;

- focus on what you are good at and work with clients who are the right fit for you and your business;

- grow your reputation by being a good referrer;

- learn technical and soft skills from other professionals;

- enhance your business resilience;

- build a community and enjoy your work.

We will explore each of these while setting out how to create a referral strategy tailored to you. You may think that a strategy is unnecessary, because referrals flow inevitably from having a good reputation. Do impressive work, build a reputation and the referrals will follow. Unfortunately, the world is a more competitive and complicated place than that. You have to be proactive and strategic. In this book we set out how to reliably bring in quality clients that stay loyal to build your career and grow your business.

After reading *Working with Strangers*, you will be able to identify the different types of referral partner and know how to work with them. You will know how to make trusted partners out of strangers, avoid common mistakes, and feel comfortable in making and receiving referrals. You will be confident in exploiting your website and marketing budget as part of your referral strategy. You'll use technology to reinforce human interactions, not replace them.

The lessons here apply to all size of service businesses, whether freelancers, small businesses or large corporate firms. They apply across all services, from marketing to recruitment, from builders to brokers. The lessons come from many different sectors too. This book presents case studies from a social media agency, lawyers, a business consultant, a marketing expert, a journalist, an events organiser, a start-up founder and a consultant in search engine optimisation. We have found that adopting techniques from other sectors and professions makes you stand out in your own. You do not have to do anything new to be an innovator.

To ensure we are building on firm foundations, we will first examine the structural problems inherent in working with strangers, even within large organisations. We will see clues about how humans can adjust our thinking to collaborate more effectively and the importance of trust in collaboration.

Then we look in more detail at the two categories of referral: the straightforward fire-and-forget referrals and complex referrals. Most referrals will be in the first category, but we hope that the more you collaborate, the more confidence you will have to make complex referrals. By giving service providers the power to choose to work together on different projects, complex referrals are at the heart of a thriving collaboration economy.

It takes two to tango, so we devote a chapter looking at who you are and how you work, and another looking at your ideal client. To build trusting relationships, there needs to be real connection based on personality and reciprocal business need. Referrals are a tool to grow your business, but they are based on people, so a successful referral strategy must put humanity at its heart.

For the next five chapters, we focus on how to build that strategy. First, we look at the metrics that help set the direction of your strategy. These give you something to aim for and measurable ways to improve your approach. We look at how to identify your best referrers, see existing clients in a whole new light and build long-term strategic relationships.

When you put referrals front and centre, the focus of your business shifts. This is nowhere truer than in your approaches to marketing and networking, which should be geared towards generating referrals as much as finding clients directly.

We emphasise the importance of people in your referral strategy, but this poses an inherent challenge. You can only be in one place at a time, so it is hard to scale. Technology is vital for a referral strategy to succeed, provided that it augments personal connections.

Finally, we look at how to stop the self-sabotage that undermines even the best referral strategy. Only by understanding what we're doing wrong can we build a strategy that is sustainable and delivers results that allow you to thrive.

Referral strategies involve rethinking how we do business, but, if we pause for a moment, we see that the humble referral has been hiding in plain sight. It was always there, but much neglected. We hope *Working with Strangers* gives it a well-deserved place in the sun.

1

TRUST, BUT VERIFY

Before we jump into building a referral strategy, we need to understand the difficulties inherent in working with strangers. There are systemic obstacles to collaboration which are baked into modern economy and society. Humans are instinctive collaborators, but these obstacles cause trust issues.

The more people you work with, the greater the opportunity for misunderstanding and for trust to break down. There is an increased scope for bad actors, delay, mistakes, corruption, group think and cover-ups. Imagine a graph with the number of humans on the x-axis and complexity on the y-axis. The relationship is not linear; it is exponential. Each additional human doesn't just add one unit of complexity, they add one unit of complexity for each of the other people on the team. It is not surprising that when collaborating, things can fall apart, and fast.

Most of us do not deal in matters of life and death. But there is one group of professionals whose career is based on prolonging one and delaying the other. The great panoply of the medical profession, from nurses and doctors to pharmacists and physiotherapists, is involved in a daily struggle against mortality. They also routinely make referrals and collaborate with people they do not know. They are experts at working with strangers.

Or at least, they should be. The true story of a two-year-old girl's hospital experience illustrates the complexities of making referrals across large groups of strangers. Let's call her Lizzie to protect her identity; she's an ordinary happy little girl living in a village in the east of England with her family. One night in the winter of 2016, Lizzie wakes up in pain, having failed to pass urine for most of the day. She has a tummy ache so her mum, a GP trained in paediatrics, presses down on the place that hurts. Lizzie yelps not when pressure is applied, but when it is released: a classic indication of appendicitis, even if it is rare in a child this young.

Lizzie's mum takes her to hospital. By this point, the little girl is in a lot of pain and the doctors in the accident and emergency department agree that it could be appendicitis. They admit Lizzie to a surgical ward. But the surgeons think she is just too young and that the mother is overreacting. It must be something else, so they refer Lizzie to a paediatric ward.

The pain continues and Lizzie is kept in overnight. One of the paediatricians is increasingly worried that it could be appendicitis after all, so prescribes intravenous antibiotics. The paediatrician refers Lizzie for an x-ray and an ultrasound but the results come back inconclusive. The radiographer conducting the scan admits he 'is not very good at looking at paediatric scans'. Lizzie's pain starts to go away and she plays with some toys.

The following night, Lizzie deteriorates. The surgeon comes back to see her and, living up to the arrogant caricature beloved of TV drama, is haughty and dismissive of his colleagues and the worried mother. In the morning, the pain is replaced by a different kind of sickness. Her mum seeks attention from anyone who will listen. Meanwhile, inside the little girl's body, a deadly poison is slowly being absorbed into her blood stream.

This is now a race against time. Belatedly, Lizzie is scheduled to be transferred to a specialist paediatrics centre. She is given the next available ambulance and blue-lighted, sirens blaring, halfway across the country to another hospital. On arrival, however, Lizzie is seen by another surgeon. He too rejects the idea that it could be appendicitis and she spends another night on a ward. The next morning, a junior doctor sees Lizzie and orders a repeat ultrasound. It shows a perforated appendix.

Three days after she first arrived at hospital presenting with classic symptoms of appendicitis, Lizzie is finally taken to surgery. The surgeons open her up, clean away the infected material and remove her appendix. She wakes up from the general anaesthetic bleary eyed, uncomfortable but alive. She is blissfully unaware that ineffective collaboration nearly killed her.

Lessons from failure

This is not meant to be a story about medical incompetence or motherly heroics, though it is both of those. It is about when referrals go wrong and the lessons for building our own referral strategy.

It is clear from this story that even the best professionals, working in organisations built around referrals, struggle to collaborate effectively. It is tempting to think that smaller businesses without institutional support might have no chance. However, looking at this example, and the other case studies which follow in this book, there is reason to think that bigger organisations find referrals harder. For smaller businesses, a referral strategy offers a potential competitive advantage.

Organisations do not come much bigger than the United Kingdom's National Health Service, which has 1.38 million staff and is one of the ten biggest employers in the world. It is stuffed to the gills with highly trained professionals. In the UK, doctors are required to study five years for a degree, then work for two years of foundational training, before specialising for five to eight years. Training is rigorous for everyone else in the NHS too.

Not only that, but the NHS is loved. In 2012, it formed the centrepiece of the London Olympics opening ceremony. A former senior British politician once said that the NHS was 'the closest thing the English people have now to a religion'. Despite scandals and funding crises, the UK Office for National Statistics reported that in March 2022, the NHS was still the most trusted public service in the country. The NHS also has an army of bureaucrats, HR professionals and managers, as well as well-established procedures and systems, to help ensure that patients receive the best care possible. A key feature is that that medical professionals refer patients between each other, so that they are treated by the relevant specialist. If any organisation might be expected to do referrals well, it's the NHS.

In Lizzie's case, her GP mum essentially referred her to the hospital by taking her there herself, where she was seen by A&E doctors who referred her to the surgeons, who referred her to the paediatrician, who referred her, via paramedics, to a specialist paediatrics unit and more surgeons. All the people in that chain of referrals had been through a rigorous training and interview process and, between them, had decades of experience of not only working as medical professionals, but also how the system worked. They were experts in every way.

Yet it still almost ended in tragedy for the simple reason that, while collaboration is an instinct, we humans are bad at working with strangers. Our ancestors might have been able collaborate to fix a broken leg, but nowadays it is more complicated. Three lessons stand out about collaboration in the modern world.

Lesson 1: challenge your assumptions

The first is that when we are working in or interacting with institutions or complex systems, we make several assumptions. We assume that experts know what they are doing. We assume that the system works and that everyone in the system has our best interests at heart. The NHS, like large law firms, the Big Four or any multinational organisation, has a large HR department, complaints procedures and a professional culture. When we come face to face with a large organisation, there is a temptation to stop thinking and to rely on the infrastructure around us to keep us safe. The doctor, as it were, knows best.

As Lizzie's mum worked in the NHS, they were familiar with how it worked but also with its failings. They had enough knowledge to break free of their initial assumptions and challenge the system.

Bluntly, when making and receiving referrals we cannot assume our referral partners or our clients know what they are doing. We have to be on our guard.

Lesson 2: be humble, admit errors and learn from failure

For Lizzie, the first surgeon she saw was adamant that he was right. He dismissed the views of the paediatricians and Lizzie's GP mum, despite not being an expert in paediatrics. Once he had dismissed appendicitis as a possible diagnosis, it was beyond him to admit he was wrong.

In *Black Box Thinking*, Matthew Syed looks at negligence cases in hospitals, plane crashes and other disasters to analyse why things go wrong. He examines the transcripts of black box recordings, showing how co-pilots struggle to challenge the decisions of the pilot even, in one case, as he flies the plane into a mountain. Too often, Syed shows, social mores and rigid hierarchies prevent us from challenging authority and also stop us from admitting when we are wrong. They stop us learning from failure.

For our referral strategy we need to remember that humility opens our minds and keeps us willing to accept mistakes and learn from them. Frank honesty is crucial to successful collaboration because it is the starting point for trust.

Lesson 3: work on working with strangers

A key point to draw out here is that, because the NHS is so large, the doctors involved in Lizzie's story didn't know each other. They worked in a massive, faceless system, where the referral channels are set out in advance. There are only certain people in any given hospital to refer your question to and it depends on who is on shift at the time. There is no opportunity to refer work outside the system. You are forced to work with strangers.

Had the paediatrician and Lizzie's mum known the surgeon, they would have seen his arrogance for what it was. If we don't know someone, arrogance masquerades as confidence, and we doubt ourselves. As it is, all they knew were the surgeon's credentials and that the system had given him seniority and power. But in this case, that same institutional backing had fed the surgeon's overconfidence and complacency.

In Lizzie's case, her mum called a good friend of hers, a paediatric consultant working in Australia, who reaffirmed her point of view. She was able to ask for a second opinion from outside the system. The rest of us are not able to do that. She was also, for all the surgeon's condescension, an expert herself.

It takes real skill to work with strangers effectively. Communication needs to be open, direct and without ceremony. It can be ugly and scrappy, so long as the messages are received. Referral partners need to feel safe to air disagreements and challenge each other. It is therefore preferrable to know, like and trust your referral partners. But even if you do, collaboration is a skill that requires training and practice. If you want to grow your business by referrals, you will need a plan.

Trust, but verify

From the story of Lizzie's brush with death, we start to see the themes that will recur in this book. While necessary in large organisations, processes and departmental structures can hinder the referral process by impeding the building of real trust. Hierarchies can encourage arrogance and complacency. We are forced to work with strangers, rather than people we know. We often have no choice in the experts we consult, because we have to follow the path paved for us by the organisation. We should not take for granted that working with strangers is easy. We see that collaboration is a skill that requires studying.

Trusting each other is not simple either. Sociologists have identified two types: cognitive trust and affective trust. The former is the reasoned trust we have towards colleagues that they will do their job well and on time. Affective trust, meanwhile, is the deeper, heart-led trust, built on emotional connection. We have cognitive trust that a system will work and that laws will be enforced, but affective trust that our friends will be there for us in a crisis. It is complicated further because cultures place different emphasis on these types of trust. In some, it is important to build affective trust before doing business, often by dining and drinking together. In others, trust is more cognitive and transactional, based on competence and reliability, focused on the boardroom not the restaurant. Collaborating across these concepts of trust is difficult.

One response to the complexities of collaboration and trust is to rely more heavily on technology. Rather than collaborate with people, we ask artificial intelligence for help. Instead of trusting institutions with our money, we hold crypto, relying on the trustless blockchain. In place of trusting neighbours and colleagues with whom we are safe to disagree constructively, algorithms sift us into silos and echo chambers. In an efficient world, there is no place for trust. Thankfully, our human weaknesses mean we will never live in a wholly efficient world: technology is unstoppable, but collaboration and trust will be necessary so long as humans walk the earth.

Further than that, we are called to trust each other. Collaboration would not be possible if we are required to second guess everyone we work with. In *Talking to Strangers*, Malcolm Gladwell argues that trust is humanity's default position. To talk with strangers at all, we can't assume the worst. To survive as a species, we have to default to truth. Gladwell looks at the surprising number of cases of trained spy catchers being tricked by double agents, because even spy catchers assume the traitors are telling the truth (often in the face of compelling evidence). Even for spies, our instinct to trust is hard to counter. Fortunately, most of us never have to identify a mole and defaulting to trust is not naive but sensible.

In business, we must be proactive and decide who to trust. But how do we decide to trust someone we don't know? The decisions we make depend, counterintuitively, on how vulnerable we feel. We are more likely to trust others when we need them in some way. Daniel Coyle explores this idea in *The Culture Code*:

> Normally, we think about trust and vulnerability the way we think about standing on solid ground and leaping into the unknown: first we build trust, then we leap. But science is showing us that we've got it backward. Vulnerability doesn't come after trust, it precedes it. Leaping into the unknown, when done alongside others, causes the solid ground of trust to materialise beneath our feet.

So not only are we geared towards trusting strangers, but we are prone to trust them if we are vulnerable and don't know what we are doing. In other words, we have evolved to trust people because we have to: we need their help. When making a referral, we are by definition partially ignorant, otherwise we would do the work ourselves. We are vulnerable because we are putting our reputation on the line. It is the process itself which helps build trust; it is self-reinforcing.

Sometimes trust is the wrong decision. There is an old Russian proverb, made famous by Ronald Reagan in the 1980s during nuclear arms reduction talks with Mikhail Gorbachev. It implores us to 'trust, but verify'. In other words, we should trust generously, but only up to a certain point. Notable here is that Reagan came from an American culture where the word trust usually refers to the cognitive transactional kind, whereas Gorbachev is likely to have understood it to mean the deeper, affective trust more common to Russian culture. When collaborating, we will need both cognitive and affective trust. We will need to trust that our referral partners can do their job and we should also be open to forming deeper bonds of trust with them too. Either way, we should gather information on our partners and update our opinion as the facts change, because sometimes our trust will be misplaced. Let both interpretations of 'trust, but verify' be our guide as we build our referral strategy.

Growing a new business through referrals

Jack Lineker, socialed

Jack Lineker, co-founder of socialed, a social-media-led digital marketing agency, shows how a business can be built from scratch on the back of a good referral strategy. Starting the agency as a side project while still at university, in three years he has grown the business to a team of six with clients like Pro Hunter, Berkeley Group and Solo Coffee.

His biggest initial challenge was building a reputation and network from nothing. Without experience, securing work was tricky. He was strategic, identifying clients who would give him access to their network. He worked at a discount for a well-connected management consultant, who recommended him to her contacts. He then provided additional discounts for each successful referral, spurring early client acquisition.

Armed with experience and the beginnings of a portfolio, he targeted what he calls 'niches with communities', such as tradespeople and motorsports. The niche means his clients and referral partners know exactly what he does, while referrals are more common within tight-knit communities. It also means that his ongoing work for one client is visible to other potential clients. Some clients take years to land, but prospects who go silent sometimes come back because they know the same people and continue to see content produced by socialed. Working within communities means he can ask his clients directly whether they know others in their network who might benefit from his services.

Jack says his big early break came from a referral through social media. A contact spotted an Instagram story from the sportswear brand, Under Armour, who were looking for an agency for a behind-the-scenes shoot. That contact responded to the story, recommending socialed for the job. Jack jumped at the chance and Under Armour became a key client, opening doors to other brands. This is the archetypal social media referral and shows the value of having referral partners who know and understand what you do.

Social networks like Instagram and LinkedIn are great places to find referrals more generally. Production companies commonly assemble teams by putting out requests on social media, so Jack and his team must catch the opportunities as they arise. As his experience with Under Armour shows, it helps to have referral partners who spot them for him too. Another trick that works well is commenting on clients' LinkedIn posts to be seen by their network. Partly this is in the nature of what they do: social media is their business and being good at it is itself reputation enhancing.

Many businesses, particularly those not run by digital natives, do not make the most of social media for referrals. They default to using their websites and in-person networking. Has social media been a better source of referrals than his website though? 'Absolutely,' says Jack.

2

FIRE-AND-FORGET REFERRALS

The majority of referrals are simple affairs, which follow the formulation we mentioned in the Introduction: referral = recommendation + introduction. We call this classic situation the fire-and-forget referral because you don't have to think much about it once you have made the referral. Like a guided missile system, the referrer launches the referral and the recipient guides the work to completion without further input from the referrer.

If you are the recipient of a fire-and-forget referral, you receive the introduction and everything else is up to you. You quote, complete the work and bill independently of the person who made the referral. The referral of Under Armour to socialed described above was this type of referral. Jack's friend had no further input in the process once the recommendation had been made.

This chapter will break down the stages of this journey, because it is a bit more involved than it first appears. To ensure a smooth referral process, the referrer needs to fire the referral in the right direction. Even though they are not managing the client's work, the referrer should also not completely forget about the referral, but follow up to ensure it worked out. Meanwhile, there is much that recipients have to do to ensure that fire-and-forget referrals hit their mark.

Fire-and-forget v complex referrals

First, we need to establish whether a fire-and-forget referral or a complex referral is required. Does the contact just want to be introduced to a third party or do they want you to project manage? This is particularly pertinent if the contact is your client.

Service providers who prefer the fire-and-forget approach don't like asking this question. We want to focus on what we are good at and don't want to be stuck in the middle between client and third parties. It is time consuming and project management comes with risk. But your job is to add value so before you proceed, discuss this with the person asking for the referral. Be upfront: project management isn't free. It's a complex job and adds value, particularly for inexperienced clients. If they confirm they only want a recommendation and an introduction, you are making a fire-and-forget referral.

Programming the fire-and-forget referral

A guided missile is an expensive piece of kit. The military does not fire them into the air and hope for the best. They can only forget about the missile because of the work that goes into the software allowing it to lock onto the target. Your clients and contacts, likewise, are valuable assets and their work should only be sent on its way when you are locked on to the target. In the case of referrals, the target is the client's objective: know what they want to achieve and that will determine to whom you introduce them.

When making referrals, it can be tempting to focus on our own needs, such as who we like working with or favours we need to repay, rather than the needs of the client. Like the surgeon in chapter 1, it is tempting to assume that we know best because we are the experts. However, whether a referral works ultimately depends on the client. They need to like and trust the person to whom they are being referred.

As a referrer you are like the person who sets friends up on a blind date. Making a good match requires knowing the two parties well. You might know that one wants children and the other hates kids, so you know they are not a good fit. In one way, a referral is harder than matchmaking. It probably won't be informed by years of friendship and you have less time to dedicate to it. You have plenty of work to be doing, other than referring work out to third parties that does not directly benefit you. Referrals are tricky because you are dealing with at least two other parties, one of whom you might not know well.

Target locked: what are your client's priorities?

When picking a service provider, clients have to choose which two of good price, good quality and fast delivery to prioritise. This is known as the impossible triangle because they cannot have all three, despite what we service providers tell ourselves. Think of any of your clients and you will know which two they focus on. It is stressful to work for clients who want low-quality work fast and cheap, because it's hard to do anything other than your best work. Resist taking on these clients or inflicting them on any of your referral partners.

Even if you know the client well, do not assume which of these has priority before making the referral. The work is, by definition, outside your skill set. If you ask the direct question, 'do you want this work done well or quickly?', you will sound sarcastic and won't impress your client. Instead:

- For clients who appear to prioritise speed or price over quality, say: 'it seems that [speed/price] is the priority here, rather than a belt-and-braces approach?'

- For clients who apparently prioritise low price over speed: 'it seems that the right price is key here, rather than meeting a specific deadline?'

- For clients who prioritise speed over everything: 'it seems that the deadline is the overriding point here, so your work will need to be prioritised over other work, which may push up the price'.

The phrase, 'it seems that', is a great way to show you have been listening to them while allowing them to easily contradict you without any social awkwardness. If they do contradict you, that's great, because you have corrected your assumption and it will be easier to find the right referral partner for the client. It will draw out any contradictions in their thinking. Clients always want quality work fast and at a low price so asking them to prioritise helps them manage their own expectations. Your referral partner will be grateful.

Coming in hot: qualification of referrals

The client's priorities set the direction, but targets move. As a referrer it is your job to ask simple questions to determine whether the referral is a hot referral where help is needed now or whether there are dependencies and contingencies which make the referral more speculative. This is a form of lead qualification.

There are several common lead qualification methodologies out there that contain insights for qualifying referrals. IBM's BANT framework stands for budget, authority, need and timeline. When making referrals, we need a slightly different lead-qualification approach. The language of lead qualification doesn't quite work when talking about valued clients and referrals, rather than sales. Rather than lead qualification, we need referral qualification.

If you care about your reputation, you care about referral qualification. Your referral partner needs to know early that the work is coming in order to fit it into their work pipeline. On the other hand, you don't want to set hares running unnecessarily. If you send time-wasting referrals to your referral partners, it undermines your reputation and makes it less likely that you will receive referrals in the future. However, even if you are taking a small referral fee, referrals are not your main business, so the qualification process needs to be efficient.

To quickly determine whether a person is a hot referral or a future referral, let's look at the biggest dependencies and contingencies responsible for delays, scope creep and cost overruns. From our experience in assisting legal referrals around the world, we have developed the BTOP method of referral qualification, which stands for: budget, team, other parties and planning

These BTOP questions qualify potential clients as hot referrals who need help now and are willing to pay for it, before you introduce them to your referral partner. If the person is not ready, hold off making the referral.

- **Budget**: if a client does not have budget for the work that needs doing, they are wasting everyone's time. To flush out if this is an issue, say: 'a good quality [SEO consultant] is worth paying for. Does it make sense to refer you at this stage of your plans?' Do not ask if the client has budget, but highlight the cost so they know they would be wasting their time if they can't afford it.

- **Team**: without the right team in place, a client may not be ready for you to introduce them to your referral partners. If your client wants you to recommend a plumber to fit a new shower in his house but has not yet discussed it with his wife, he is not ready for the referral: the team is not aligned. To find out whether the client's team is in place and ready, ask 'is there anyone else that needs to sign off on this?' and 'are there any other referrals you need from me to complete this work?' It reveals whether there are gaps in the client's team while maintaining your positive, helpful approach. You might then recommend a different type of service provider that they need first.

- **Other parties**: it's useful to have a sense of how other parties in the process are behaving. If a client needs approval from a government agency or has yet to find a buyer for their company, for example, it might be best to wait before making a referral. General open questions are best here: 'what is your sense of the [planning department's] approach?' and 'what is the buyer's timeframe?' These reveal whether the third party is unresponsive, aggressive or unreliable. If the planning department is not responding to emails, it's likely that the client doesn't need the interior decorator just yet.

- **Planning**: the state of the client's own planning is key to spotting a hot referral. If the client is only thinking in broad terms or has contradictory goals, they are not ready for a referral. Ask, 'what stage are you at with this work?' to reveal whether the client has just started and needs some help figuring out what their plan is or has a specific task that needs to be done.

If you ask these questions and think the contact is ready, tell the referral partner the information you have discovered. Send this by email copying in the client and the referral partner, so your client can see how much you are taking care of them and the referral partner can hit the ground running.

BTOP qualification will enhance your reputation in your community and put you top of everyone's list of favourite referrers. All sides will remember how easy it is doing business with you, which will encourage them to refer work back to you in future.

Identify the right referral partner

The selection of the right service provider is where a referrer comes into their own. It's the part that a directory, website or AI cannot do. By selecting a particular referral partner for a particular client, you are performing a nuanced and delicate task, taking into account your knowledge of both.

Identify what your referral partners do and what work they want to receive. We are not experts in every area of work, so the nuance of another person's profession will not always be obvious to us. If you are in doubt, ask them. Ask if they have the time, given their other commitments, to take on the work. Once you have the all clear from the referral partner, you're ready to launch your fire-and-forget referral by making the introduction.

What steps should you take when receiving a referral?

We are now going to look at a fire-and-forget referral from the point of view of the service provider receiving the referral. It's your job to help the referral to reach the target, which is the realisation of the client's objective. As with any of your other clients, this will comprise providing high-quality, good-value service and communicating well. But if the client has come through as a fire-and-forget referral, extra steps are needed.

The difficulty for you as the recipient of a referral is that the referrer takes on some of the characteristics of a client, rather than just a fellow service provider. The referrer doesn't have your expertise to spot the issues that could cause delays and extra cost. That is why they are making a referral to you. Like a client, this lack of knowledge can make them overly optimistic. A referrer's mentality becomes, 'I don't know what the problem is, so there is no problem'. Rather than help manage a client's expectations, some referrers heighten them instead.

As the recipient of the referral, you want to make a good impression and land the work so you may be inclined to minimise problems too. You won't have all the documents and backstory, or know how much handholding the particular client needs. Some clients are more demanding than others. Scoping and quoting are hard, and will be wildly inaccurate without good information. But the temptation is not to ask too many questions to land the client quickly, so you overpromise. Sure enough, high expectations are dashed and the client looks around for someone to blame.

Thankfully, it is straightforward to avoid this situation. If the person making the referral has not followed the BTOP referral qualification steps, do this yourself. Wasting time on uncertain future referrals is frustrating, distracts you from profitable work and deters you from collaborating in future. As you do not know the client, asking the BTOP questions on email will appear unfriendly, ungrateful or overly formulaic. Book a quick scoping call with them to flush out their priorities and determine if they are a hot referral.

Once you are certain that the client is a hot referral, follow a simple checklist to land the client:

- Double check the initial and final deadlines with the client. If you hit the initial deadlines, like the delivery of a scoping report or scheduling a kick-off call, you start off on the right foot. The final deadline will allow you to schedule other work around it and to plan.

- Ensure you have the skills and capacity to do the work. Sometimes a referrer will have misunderstood what you do. If it is not where your expertise lies or not the direction that you want to take your business, then turn down the work politely and set out what it is you actually do, so that they know for next time.

- Set up a call with the referrer, however small the piece of work is. Show you care. Ask what the client's fee expectations are. It is hard to ask the client this question, but much easier to ask another service provider, particularly as the referrer won't want you to make them look too expensive or cheap. Express this as 'I want to make sure our approach and fees are aligned'.

- Send out the quote to the client directly. The referrer does not usually want to have to check your quotes so have confidence and send these to the client directly, copying in the referrer.

- If the client does not reply to the quote, follow up with them three days later and then weekly for a month. There is no excuse for failure to chase a potential client: once you have sent the quote, the person is only one step away from instructing you, which is the closest thing to a client they can be. Keep the referrer copied into the email chain to add social pressure on the client to respond, even if it is just to tell you they have instructed another service provider. It also shows the referrer that you are a reliable and efficient referral partner.

- If the client instructs you, put the client through your onboarding procedures as quickly as possible. For professional firms, it is an involved process of anti-money laundering and other checks. For others, it is much simpler, but either way make the process efficient, tech driven and systematic. Slick admin is your first opportunity to demonstrate competence.

- Do not step on the toes of the referrer. Do not steal clients. Except in extreme circumstances, don't openly contradict the referrer. Have disagreements politely one to one behind the scenes.

Forget fire and forget: fire and follow up instead

Once the work has been referred, it is not over for the referrer either. Take the opportunity to build your professional reputation and the quality of your referral network by following up with a quick email or a short, standardised survey to the client, asking how well the referral partner has responded to their needs.

Send out the survey automatically one month after you have made a referral and store the responses in your CRM (customer relationship management) tool. You'll gradually build up a better picture of your referral partners.

The survey should ask the following questions about the recipient service provider on a scale of one to ten:

- How likely are you to recommend them?

- How would you rate the quality of their work?

- How commercial and pragmatic are they?

- How easy was their onboarding process?

- How responsive are they?

The results will give you a golden opportunity to improve your own service. If the person to whom you're sending the survey is also your client, you can send them the same survey about your own service, permitting a direct comparison. This is uniquely valuable information.

Once the results are in, arrange a catch-up with the client to discuss the results. Drill down into their responses, learn about yourself and your referral partners, and nail down the client's loyalty to you. Note down the words and phrases they use to describe you. These are the words and phrases you then use in your marketing material.

This follow-up will set you apart from other service businesses. So if you want to make the most of this type of referral, it's not quite fire and forget, more fire and follow up.

3

COMPLEX REFERRALS

As a reminder, a complex referral = recommendation + introduction + teamwork. People often miss that complex referrals exist at all. When thinking of referrals, we imagine fire-and-forget referrals. When discussing teamwork, we think of working with colleagues and friends. Even in the medical profession, where they use the word referral when moving patients around the system, doctors still think of each other as colleagues rather than referral partners.

We look at it another way: where a client starts their journey with one expert who then works together with another for that client, we call it a complex referral. For example, when I am working on the sale of a company, as a corporate lawyer, it is my role to fill in any gaps in the client's team of advisers. I assemble service providers across different countries and practice areas, from tax lawyers and accountants to valuers and notaries, and then work with them all on the project. We become, temporarily, teammates. When relationships are seen in this light, it highlights that there are two processes involved: referrals and teamwork. As we have seen, simple referrals involve skill and experience; building and maintaining highly functioning teams is more challenging still. Looked at like this, it is clear that the combination of referral and teamwork requires careful thought.

Whether inside or outside an organisational structure, a team of referral partners can lack leadership, cohesion and accountability. If things go wrong, it is difficult to know who is responsible or accountable. Often no one is incentivised to manage the project and matters can drift. Service providers tend to stick to their silo, so no one sees the big picture. It takes time to get to know the rest of the team. Even within the same organisation, advisers are increasingly in different locations, with different office hours and lack a cohesive office culture. Correspondence takes time, decisions go round in circles. A team is only as strong as its weakest link, broken by one dud team member. If the project manager isn't alive to it, there will be delays and dispute. The collaboration will likely fail.

Complex referrals are not something that can be avoided. They are everywhere in business, but do we not pay them the attention they deserve, which means they are more difficult than they should be. These struggles deter us from regularly working in teams across and between organisations. It represents a lost opportunity: rather than collaborate with other experts, we dabble outside our skill set, fail to become true specialists and serve smaller clients. If we really want to grow our businesses through referrals, far from avoiding complex referrals, we should embrace them.

In this chapter we will look at what makes a great complex referral and how you can take on the project management role to become a lynchpin of the collaboration economy. Successful complex referrals require:

- Effective project management

- Great communication

- Decent team members

Let's look at each of these in the context of making and receiving referrals.

The project manager

Few work situations are more stressful than working on a project that is managed incompetently. In complex referrals, where no one seizes the role, the project manager will usually be the client or the service provider who has known the client the longest. In large organisations, the client partner will be the relationship manager but may not want to be the project manager. They are responsible for gladhanding and fielding complaints but not managing the project. If someone does end up taking on the project management role, it's unlikely they will have project management experience or training.

Make no mistake: project management is a skill in its own right. It is distinct from leadership. The direction of the work should be set by the client. The job of project manager is to implement. If the client is king, the project manager is the prime minister.

As a corporate lawyer, I have frequently seen clients who lack project management experience try to take on the role. They do not see team building or project management as something worth paying for, so they have a go themselves. When a client builds their own team of referral partners, this is similar to a complex referral and the client is analogous to the referrer. Where a client brings you on board in this situation, the temptation is not to rock the boat. But the client is not really looking to be the project manager. What they want is the project to be completed successfully, they just don't know or trust anyone enough to be lead it.

On the other hand, where the client does trust a service provider to be the project manager, it is likely to be a longstanding trusted adviser who, like the client, lacks project management experience. As that service provider may be the person who has referred you the work in the first place, you are not incentivised to challenge their position as project manager. You will be socially, if not financially, in their debt. Here is what often happens:

- Your contract with the client does not include project management and is on a tight estimate or fixed fee.

- The client or lead adviser, who is not an expert at project management and does not enjoy it, does no project management and the work starts to drift and costs rise.

- If you are proactive and conscientious, you end up as the project manager, doing perceived low-value work that you have not included in your quote and struggle to charge for.

It's a miserable result. To avoid it, if the matter relates principally to your area of expertise, consider if you should be the project manager. Ask who is currently managing the project and for them to organise a kick-off call with all the service providers and the client.

Ask the client or the lead service provider how much project management they want you to do. Make it clear how much work is involved in project management, so that they are held accountable when they turn out to be bad at it. Ascertain from the project manager:

- Will they arrange regular calls with the team?

- Will they keep track of everything that needs doing and the dependencies between items on the to-do list?

- Will they be responsible for chasing and keeping the team accountable?

On the call with all of the service providers, agree that one of you is going to produce a steps plan by a certain date. The question will flush out who wants to be the project manager.

If it is not you, you will need to manage up. Treat the project manager as the client relationship manager and in some ways your boss. Keep them informed of your work and ask open questions about other areas. Stay curious and you might remind them to do something they haven't done. If you find yourself falling into the project management role, reprise the conversation; having raised project management as an issue at the start, you have permission to hold your client or the lead adviser to account later on.

Project management

If you become the project manager of a complex referral, the buck stops with you. Even if there isn't a legal straight line from another service provider's incompetence to your insurance, you are in charge and are morally accountable to your client. If things fall apart, it is your responsibility to clean up the mess. The client doesn't care about excuses. They want the job done and they hired you to do it.

Now consider what good looks like: what is the outcome your client wants and how might this be measured? Consider what it is that you want too: a smiling client, a great testimonial, fees paid without quibble. When planning out the project, rather than starting at the beginning, work back from this desired end point. It will help you visualise everything that needs to be done.

The steps plan

It is unlikely that you will be trained in project management or the use of Gantt charts. If you find yourself frequently project managing, this training will be worth it. Otherwise, we recommend using a steps plan. In my career, I have seen law firms use many versions on the other side in transactions. It often turns out to be the most important document in any project.

The steps plan needs to make it clear at a glance what is outstanding and who is responsible. It should include actions to be completed, as well as any deliverables and documents to be prepared. It is the bible of the project as you go along. Everything should be in it. An example of what this looks like is included as an appendix, based on over a decade of managing complex transactions.

You may be tempted by interactive and collaborative project management tools. Use these to communicate with the team and assign tasks, but do not forget the steps plan. For collaboration to work, there needs to be a single point of authority, a single source of truth that is not collaborative. One person should control the steps plan: the project manager. They may have an assistant who updates the document, but the project manager is responsible for keeping the steps plan up to date. No one else in the team should edit the document. The perfect steps plan should:

- Be saved privately. You control access to the document so do not save it where others can edit it.

- Include a definitions section, including all the people involved on the transaction, ideally with their contact details.

- Be a landscape word processor document, because it is going to include a lot of text. Excel spreadsheets work for tables but not for paragraphs.

- Be a table with six columns including these headings: number, document or action, deadline, responsibility, signatories and notes.

- Be split into rows under different sub-headings, which will vary depending on the project. Each subheading should be given a corresponding letter. Whatever the project, the first two subheadings should be: (A) research and preliminaries and (B) approvals. The last section should be devoted to post-completion filings and notifications. Do not leave out this section: it's often the most important part.

- Number each deliverable or action, starting at one under each subheading. The numbering must be automatic, so that deliverables or actions can be added to each subsection without upsetting the numbering system for the whole steps plan.

It is an intentionally analogue solution in a digital world. Nothing else will give you the control to manage a complex referral and bring the project to a successful conclusion. So, how do you use the steps plan to manage a team?

At the beginning of the day, save a new copy of the steps plan with the date at the end of the document name. Write the date in reverse order (so that 16 January 2024 becomes 20240116). All saved copies will list in date order and the current one will be easier to find in the folder where they are saved. Do not discard old copies.

- Use it as a living document. Update it as information comes in. It only works if it is up to date and reliable.

- Rather than keeping separate attendance notes of meetings with other advisers and the client, keep everything together by writing updates into the notes section of the steps plan.

- Arrange regular calls to run through the steps plan with the client and the team. It will stop team members from forgetting about the little things and encourage them to speak out if they spot balls being dropped.

- All this information is hard to read, so colour code each item on the steps plan according to its status. I use seven colours, from yet to start to completed, but fewer may work for you. The more granular, the easier it is to see at a glance what needs doing. It keeps meetings efficient as you can see what has yet to be started and skip over the completed items.

- At the end of the day (or longer timeframe depending on the pace of the transaction), email the steps plan to the team with any questions you have for them. Make it clear each time that no one else is to amend the document. You do not want two versions of the same document.

It is old fashioned, but it works.

Communication

Working with strangers is particularly hard because you will not have a base level of common cultural touch points or opinions. Add in large teams, different languages and nationalities, and it becomes doubly difficult, as you might have different ways of thinking, sharing negative feedback, persuading or leading. Get it wrong and you will demotivate, offend and confuse. Erin Meyer's *The Culture Map: Breaking through the invisible boundaries of global business* goes into detail of what to expect when working with different cultures. She recommends:

> On a multicultural team, you can save time by having as few people in the group work across cultures as possible. For example, if you are building a global team that includes small groups of participants from four countries, choose one or two people from each country – the most internationally experienced of the bunch – to do most of the cross-cultural collaboration. Think carefully about your larger objectives before you mix cultures up. If your goal is innovation or creativity, the more cultural diversity the better, as long as the process is managed carefully. But if your goal is simple speed and efficiency, then monocultural is probably better than multicultural.

One rule is the same whether you are in a monocultural group or a small team: clarity is vital. Make sure you communicate clearly what you want to happen and by when. Bear in mind that this approach may in itself be confounding for people in some cultures who are used to reading between the lines and drawing inferences. Sending around action points at the end of a meeting might be interpreted as patronising or distrustful, implying that they don't know how to do their job. But here clarity is your friend too: state at the outset that as you are managing a cross-cultural team, you will be explicit to avoid confusion and that no offence is meant.

Pay particular attention to communication when referral partners have different first languages. Even bilingual people will miss cultural references and idioms, and it can be embarrassing to make errors of grammar and vocabulary. When learning French in Lyon some years ago, I confidently challenged a fellow treadmill user to '*faire les courses*'. Sadly I was out by a couple of letters and had inadvertently asked him to go shopping (I meant '*faire la course*', of course). The more complex referrals you are involved in, the more likely it is that you will find yourself working regularly with service providers and clients in their second language, so be patient and tolerant.

Keep an eye out for whether the person you are talking to has understood. Rephrase sentences to avoid certain words that might not be commonly known. Use fewer and simpler words, because the more and the longer you use, the harder the listener's brain has to work. Remember that just because someone doesn't have the same level of vocabulary as you do does not make them stupid, bad at their job or rude. After meetings, the project manager should send around the action points in writing and ask for comments. This will flush out any misunderstandings and also keep people accountable.

Avoid making assumptions about your referral partners, which includes their political views, religion, sexuality, gender and their level of education. As such, it's even more important than usual to keep your views neutral. Unveil your personality and viewpoints gradually.

Do not be boorish and inflict your opinions on people uninvited. Be polite.

The process of collaboration enhances trust and trust facilitates collaboration. The same is true for communication. Whether you are the project manager or just a member of the team, speak to the other service providers and the client as often as you can. Good communication helps you to get to know, like and trust each other, while getting to know, like and trust each other makes it much easier to communicate.

The team and legacy advisers

As a member of a team working on a large project, you may have the opportunity to recommend other service providers to assist. This is your opportunity to be a link in the complex referral chain. Recommend those providers you know, like and trust. You'll augment your own reputation with the client and get to work with a trusted partner on a large transaction. The more members of the team you are responsible for introducing, the better. You will be working with familiar faces and enjoy the process more.

However, in the same way that employees do not choose their colleagues, in complex referral situations we rarely choose all our teammates. We can all think of incompetent colleagues whose mistakes or laziness have impacted our work lives in some way. In complex referral situations, you will come across other service providers who are already advising your client. We call them legacy advisers.

Some legacy advisers are great. They are already familiar with the client so they can read you in, provide documents and answer questions quickly. But working with legacy advisers can also be painful, particularly if they are lacking the necessary expertise, are poor communicators or insist on project managing when they are unable to do so. There can be a status issue: the legacy adviser might be defensive of their position as the top dog. They may be insecure in their own abilities and condescending or dismissive of reasonable questions from the new service provider joining the team.

If you find yourself on a team with the bad sort of legacy adviser, inform the client so that they have the opportunity to fix it. As you do not know the strength of the relationship, be delicate in how you approach the subject. Have the conversation on the phone or in person and avoid insults. Explain what is required for the project to work and focus on how the legacy adviser is not meeting that requirement rather than any inherent skill gap or character deficiency. Then provide a solution. This will either involve you taking on a particular role or recommending other service providers to take their place. If the client disagrees with your advice, so be it. They are on notice, which will make the situation easier to rectify subsequently.

Tying up the loose ends

Whether it's building a house or selling a company, there is usually a moment in a project when it feels like the hard work is over. The adrenaline fades. The tense negotiations are resolved. If you are the project manager, your job is far from done.

The post-completion administrative matters should be in your steps plan, but the steps plan is useless if you stop looking at it. Forget registration deadlines, tax payments and reporting requirements at your peril. The client may still be surprised by a large bill after the main work has been completed. So after the big completion moment, arrange a call with the client to congratulate them and reinforce the relationship, while also reminding them of the work that still needs doing.

Do this right, you'll have run a perfect complex referral and you will be a model for others in the collaboration economy.

Conclusion

When done well, complex referrals are the pinnacle of collaboration, but the inherent difficulties mean that complex referrals often feel like negative experiences. They succeed if the right project manager is appointed, you use a steps plan, communicate clearly and pick the right team.

The prize for your business is the ability to work on large projects that are out of reach for you and your immediate team alone. These large projects are lucrative and open doors to work with other large clients.

By allowing smaller businesses to compete with larger organisations, complex referrals level the playing field and increase the choice for clients. Competition from smaller players might even improve the way larger organisations service their own clients.

Give referrals to receive referrals

Bill Cogan, Seven Legal

Bill Cogan, founder of Seven Legal, a London-based boutique law firm, is a master of the legal referral. His top tip is that to get referrals, you have to give referrals, which is why he is such an active member of networks like Adviserly. He explains that he adds value to his clients and potential clients by making himself useful and introducing them to other firms in other countries, even if he gets no direct benefit at the time.

Recently, a start-up founder needed Canadian corporate law advice on their fundraising documents. Seven Legal advises start-ups on their growth journey but does not advise on Canadian law, so could not take on the work themselves. Bill quickly found a Canadian firm who could help and introduced them to the potential client. The firm was similar to Seven Legal so it was a great fit for the client and the law firm.

While Seven Legal didn't get the work that time and received no referral fee for making the introduction, in under a week the same client had referred another of their contacts to Seven Legal, which became a paying client. The moral of the story? What goes around comes around and with referrals it pays to pay it forward.

4

YOUR REFERRAL
PERSONALITY TYPE

A referral strategy, more than other business growth strategies, is personal. A pay-per-click strategy does not depend on your character. Search engine optimisation does not involve bonding with website visitors. But as a referrer, it's your reputation on the line. Your aim is not to be a stranger, but to get to know, like and trust people.

We therefore need to understand who we are before tailoring a referral strategy that works for us as individuals. This chapter will identify different types of referral personality to help you understand which approaches work best for you. As we see from Bill Cogan's example at Seven Legal, some referrers take a generous and proactive approach to referrals, gregariously spreading goodwill. It works well for him, but for your referral strategy to be sustainable, it must be tailored to you. You won't implement a plan that doesn't match who you are and what you want out of your work life.

Everyone has the potential to be a great referrer because it is a skill that is learned. There is a misconception that rainmakers, those professionals who are great at bringing in new work, must be larger than life extroverts. But the best referrers can just as well be shy introverts, provided they adopt a strategy tailored to them.

Referrals are like dating, but with the stated aim of two-timing your partners. Like dating, sometimes a relationship doesn't work and it is hard to know why. At Adviserly, we see that successful referrals depend on members taking the time to get to know each other. We can work well with relatively new contacts, but it takes a long time to build deep referral relationships, even if they are polyamorous.

Whether a relationship works is a function of who we are as much as who our partner is. The first stranger we meet in the referral process is often the one in the mirror. So before finding your perfect referral partners, you need to find yourself.

There are as many different referrer personalities as there are categories of service providers. They are difficult to define: we cannot draw neat lines around someone's personality. While we are all individuals, our personalities are affected by our culture, upbringing and professional training. The aim of setting out different personality types here is to prompt reflection and provide a rule of thumb when you meet new referral partners. Everyone will exhibit behaviour across the categories and we can all change over time.

With these caveats, let's look at the personality types and the different ways we can sort them. First, we're going to categorise personalities based on motivation, specifically why people have chosen the job they have and what keeps them in it. Secondly, we're going to look at the different types of negotiator using a framework suggested by expert negotiator, Chris Voss. Then we will look at the effect culture has on the way we perceive personalities.

Personalities by motivation

They say you are what you eat, but we say you are why you work. People with different motivations will exhibit different referral behaviours. If you know what motivates both you and the person you are referring work to, you increase the chances of building a sustainable and profitable referral relationship.

The subtitle for Steven Sinek's celebrated book *Start with Why*, is *How great leaders inspire everyone to take action*. For our purposes, the action you want to inspire is collaboration in the form of referrals. To do that, you need to understand your motivations and those of your referral partners. Why do people become lawyers, accountants or any other type of professional? Why did you go into marketing? At Adviserly, we have observed three archetypes:

- The default-career professional

- The mission-led

- The obsessive

The default-career professional

People leave school or university and need something to do. At this age, a professional career involves further academic or vocational training and offers the path of least resistance. You'll learn a skill and always be employable in a big organisation, helping deliver on someone else's dream. Maybe you'll even learn to enjoy it or at least be able to convince yourself that you do. This used to be me.

We default-career professionals want referrals as part of our business development. Our ambitions follow tramlines set by people who have gone before us, so we want to grow a practice to do well at our next appraisal. We want to show how proactive we are, without being at all entrepreneurial. As this suggests, the default-career professional is a perfectly decent referral partner, but they will never be a top-flight referrer: they just don't care enough.

The mission-led

The mission-led are great referral partners if you know what their mission is, because everything they do will be geared towards a particular goal. Find out what the goal is and, assuming you share it, frame your relationship as one to enable it. You'll establish that crucial know, like and trust almost instantly. A meeting of minds like this is rare, but you can usually spot it if you are mirroring each other's language. But beware: if you are cynical about sharing a mission, you will sound like so many corporate drones. The mission-led will see through the inauthenticity.

Most of us like to think we have a mission, but few of us really do. For most, earning to provide for our families is an honourable goal in itself. It is not a mission, though. As Sinek says, profit and salary are not your purpose, they are an outcome of work and are the same for everyone.

If you are mission-led, remember that many other people are not. It is your role to bring the energy to the team. Others need to do their job: they don't need to be true believers.

The obsessives

Obsessives are people who genuinely love their subject matter. Obsessives love tax, accounts, marketing or website design to the point of being dreary about it. All professionals should at least like what they do, otherwise they should do something else. But these folk take it to another level.

If you are an obsessive, you may want to focus on your subject and therefore think that a referral strategy is not for you. On the contrary, your passion for your subject matter is a magnet to others. Once people find you, they will never let you go. Because you are rare, people will want you in their lives as the expert to turn to when they have a question. They will refer clients to you, invite you to their events and rave about you. Produce content based on the details of your expertise and let people hear about you. Don't forget to charge for the work you do.

Personalities by negotiating style

All professional relationships are at some point a negotiation. Whether you are plotting your rise to partnership or want to leverage existing contacts to obtain additional clients, you are in the business of negotiating.

In his book on negotiating, *Never Split the Difference*, Chris Voss talks about three types of negotiators: assertives, accommodators and analysts. It will help you deal with individual referral partners by establishing your and your referral partners' negotiating style.

Assertives

Assertives like to win and they like to talk. They will fill every silence by giving their point of view. Voss says:

> The assertive type believes time is money; every wasted minute is a wasted dollar ... Their self-image is linked to how many things they can get accomplished in a period of time. For them, getting the solution perfect isn't as important as getting it done.

Let's be honest, you assertives sometimes appear unpleasant. You might be a great person, but your harsh tone and blunt style is unlikely to endear you to a potential referral partner. When referring work out, you are dictatorial. When receiving work, you take over. If this sounds like you, remember that referrals are about collaboration, so try to listen more than you talk. A winner-takes-all strategy will not endear you to your referral partners.

If you must work with an assertive, Voss recommends appealing to their need for respect. Listen and show you understand them. Use what Voss calls a mirror: state back to them what they have said to you. Your goal is for the assertive to say 'that's right'. If it feels like they are trying to boss you around on fees, for example, and tell you that their client 'demands great value', mirror their language, and then pivot like this: 'it seems that your client really wants good value for this work. I offer great quality service which is great value, but it's not cheap'. By coming at it from their point of view, you earn the right to disagree.

51

Accommodators

Most of us try to be accommodating so you probably think this is a good thing to be. Some people are accommodating because they want something. Others by their nature want to accommodate all the time: like puppies wanting to be loved, they are people pleasers.

Being an accommodator is great for referrals. You are a natural at getting people to know, like and trust you. The downside is that accommodators can cause frustration: they are so determined to be liked that they fail to convey their own needs or limitations, such as a lack of time or expertise. They struggle to say no and struggle to deliver. Overpromising and underdelivering is the curse of the accommodator. The irony is that their hatred of conflict and eagerness to please causes conflict and displeasure.

If this sounds a bit like you, learn to say no without using the word. No sounds harsh to accommodators, but there are plenty of ways around it. Say something like: 'I would love to take on this referral but I have a big case on at the moment, so would not be able to give it the attention it needs for another couple of weeks'. You have continued to be accommodating, but you have said no or not now. Far better to do this than take on work you have no time to deliver.

Second, learn to convey your own needs and be confident that your views are just as important as your counterpart's. Rather than saying the client's proposed fee structure won't work, say: 'my clients love the service I provide. How can I offer your client the same service for less than I charge them?' It gets your point across but invites your counterpart to solve the problem for you. Conflict avoided.

If you are dealing with an accommodator, be sure to dig into whether they have capacity to help by asking open questions that invite them to agree with you: 'I'm really busy at the moment, how are you finding things?' Use their eagerness to agree against them to flush out if they are overworked and unable to take on the referral. If they have capacity to help, make sure you pin them down with deliverables and deadlines. List the action points at the end of a call and follow up to make sure they are on track.

Analysts

Blessed are the perfectionists for they shall inherit the earth and then endlessly worry that it isn't good enough. Many professionals are methodical and diligent; some teeter into perfectionism. Perfectionism is damaging for referrals.

As Voss describes them, analysts tend to move slowly, gather information dutifully, hate surprises and generally avoid negotiating at all if they can avoid it. Sensitive to reciprocity, they will lose trust in you quickly, if you come to meetings or send emails unprepared. They like taking things offline in order to think about them.

If you are an analyst, what are the implications for your referral relationships? You are instinctively distrustful of non-analysts, so you'll need to get to know accommodating and assertive personalities before you refer work to them. Cultural differences and approaches to timekeeping and responding to emails may be particularly frustrating for you.

Conversely, you are probably irritated by clients and referral partners who pester you for responses sooner than you are able to give them. The right answer is better than a quick answer.

If you are an analyst, think of referrals like any other complex system. You are part of the process and you have your role to play. Sometimes referrals do not result in work, so think of it as a game of percentages. You only need a small percentage to land for the process to be valuable. Start building your referral network and get to know people early.

If working with an analyst, don't pick up the phone, schedule a call. Give them plenty of time ahead of deadlines. Do what you say you are going to do and don't be offended if they don't smile at you all the time.

Personalities by culture

It is easy for outsiders to conflate your culture and your personality. We see ourselves as individuals, but others may see us as a variation on a theme of our culture. We see the trees; others see the whole wood. Our culture shapes our approach to communication and conflict, how we provide negative feedback and lead. As a Brit, for example, saying regards, instead of kind regards, at the end of an email, can evidence considerable annoyance with the recipient, which is likely to go over the heads of people from cultures with a more direct approach. When working with referral partners across cultures. it is important to know how your culture has preprogrammed you to certain ways of thinking and communicating which others may mistake for your personality.

Communicating between cultures may be challenging, but that doesn't mean you shouldn't do it, just be aware that a person's behaviour towards you may be more a result of their culture than their personality. Rather than falling out with them or taking offence, a more constructive response is to name the cultural differences and work around them. This is a complex and sensitive topic beyond the scope of this book, but Erin Meyer's *The Culture Map* provides a good guide to navigating these fraught cross-cultural waters.

Make the most of who you are

It is easy to blame other people when referrals don't work. They don't respond fast enough, their pricing is unreasonable, the client is indecisive. But as with many things in our lives, we hold the key to our success or failure.

Referrals are the best way of building a service business, and service businesses depend on the relationship between service provider and client. There are only so many clients you have capacity to take on and only so many referral partners you can know, like and trust. So it is best to take on clients referred to you by people who understand your strengths and weaknesses.

A referral strategy is built around people, not algorithms or artificial intelligence. Spend some time to think about who you are, why you do what you do and what your negotiating style is. Consider how your culture affects your way of thinking and behaving. Then reflect on what characteristics you are looking for in your referral partners and clients. Identify those personalities that you don't gel with and adapt to manage those differences. If they prove insurmountable, don't worry: it is not possible to have a great professional relationship with everyone. Learn what worked and what didn't and move on. It takes time but is a sustainable way of building a thriving professional career or service business.

So whether you are an assertive default-career professional or an obsessive analyst, you will now hopefully be thinking about the implications of your personality on building your referral strategy. The aim is to build one that plays to your strengths and allows for your weaknesses, learning how to improve or compensate for them. As we continue building that strategy, think about which tactics will work for you. Set aside the rest.

Service businesses should focus on referrals, not search engine optimisation

Jules Zeng, SEO consultant

Jules, a freelance SEO consultant from London, has what might be a surprising view of referrals. Her job is to help businesses obtain clients by improving their SEO ranking on search engines. But for her own clients, she prefers to receive referrals. Like many professional service providers, there are many people who do what Jules does. A search will reveal many people who seem to be like her. But a search tells you nothing about her quality, her approach or her style. Only a referral can do that.

She tells of a meeting with a client after she had just come in from surfing (waves, not the web). She was sitting in her car with her surfboard behind her. The client knew her well and this was their vibe too. Just at the point they were about to tell her about a referral opportunity, her phone slips from the dashboard and hits her laptop on the way down, muting the call. Eventually the client manages to get the message through and, despite the literal slip, they make the referral to a potential client anyway. This is the bond they have: they know and trust each other so well, this informal style is all part of the relationship.

The referred client gets in touch with Jules and sends across a long document that is more a full-time job description than a specification for a freelancer. Jules replies saying thank you but this is not what she does. But they are insistent: Jules has been so highly recommended that they just want to work with her. If she wants to work in a particular way, they will adjust to suit her. Jules replies and they get to know each other. Jules decides they are a great fit too and she sets out her terms. The client accepts.

Jules's example is great because it shows the power of existing clients as referrers and the power of saying no. Through existing client referrals, Jules has been able to build a thriving consultancy business that fits her life, not the other way around.

5

YOUR IDEAL CLIENT
AND VALUE PROPOSITION

Once you have figured out who you are, it's time to identify your ideal client type and what value you are offering. Think of your value proposition as the problem you are helping your client to solve or objective you are helping them reach. It is a key component in the referral strategy.

Why does this matter? When it comes to a referral strategy, the value of each potential client is high, but it takes more time to obtain each client. It is stressful to put the effort into winning referrals, only to end up with the wrong clients. Referrals are personal and in service businesses you can end up working with clients for years. If they are not a good fit, it will undermine your job satisfaction and your mental health. You will stop wanting to win new clients and do a worse job.

Imagine you're a gardener and have a great longstanding client. Some time ago you did her a favour and laid a patio for her. The client's sister then asks her for a recommendation to construct a garden wall. The client knows you are a hard worker, so you'll probably be able to build the wall for her sister. She introduces you. Do you take on the work? Do you want to be an expert gardener or do you want to do odd jobs? Building a wall requires skill that you'd have to learn as you go. Rather than being the go-to expert able to charge a premium, you become a generalist. Gardening and wall-building are different skills and are hard to package together for clients in a cohesive message.

Instead, follow Jules Zeng's example, be clear about your value proposition and don't dabble. Her story shows what it looks like when you get this right. She was so confident in her value proposition and how she wanted to work that she could say no repeatedly until the client adjusted their requirements around her. If we are going to live up to our potential as great collaborators, we must collaborate with the right clients on the right projects.

The power of niches

If you can identify your ideal client and value proposition, your referral strategy will flow smoothly from that. If you can't, how will your referral partners know who to refer to you? If you provide a muddled range of services, even your former clients might not have a great idea what it is you do or how well you do it. Your referral strategy will work better if you have a niche.

It is easier to know your target client and value proposition if you are a specialist or operate in a particular sector or for particular clients. It can feel counterintuitive and scary to niche down; if you eat what you kill, it feels safer to eat everything. A young business has to make it from day to day and you don't have the luxury of being picky. But being omnivorous presents a confusing picture for potential referrers. We saw from Jack Lineker's story at socialed that once you have your practice off the ground, you can specialise quickly for target client types with particular problems or goals.

If your value proposition is vague, your referral partners won't think of you when someone asks them for a referral. If they have to double check what it is that you do, they might not bother. If there is any risk that you might be in competition with them, a great potential referral partner will think twice before making an introduction. Your referral partners are busy people, so any uncertainty can be the difference between a successful and unsuccessful referral. If your website advertises you as the jack of all trades, you appear to be the master of none.

In your niche though, a crystal-clear value proposition will put you in the front of your referrers' minds when someone asks them for a recommendation. By working only with your target clients, you will be able to convert those referrals more effectively. Your initial meetings with the client will flow naturally. Your questions will identify the main issues quickly. Your experience and confidence will shine through. If you regularly work for specific types of clients on particular types of work, your quotes will be more accurate. You will know what fees different types of client are happy to pay, as well as how long or complex a particular job will be.

Client personas

To identify your niche we need to think about your ideal client and what they need. This process starts by defining your client personas. Client or customer personas are archetypes of your clients with particular traits, such as behaviour, geographic location or demography. These are fictionalised and idealised versions of real people or businesses. They help you to think about the types of clients you have, clarify your branding and tailor your services.

Typically, client personas are segmented into:

- Geography

- Demography

- Personality

- Behaviour

For B2B service providers, we can also add:

- Sector

- Size and growth prospects of the client business

- Job title or role within the client

Other categories will be relevant for your business, depending on the services it provides and the sector it is in. For the gardening example above, personas could be segmented by the size of the client's garden or whether their house is a terrace or detached. On the other hand, divorce lawyers care about more about their prospect's marital status, while estate agents might have personas based on whether they are first-time or cash buyers.

Client personas are key to shaping your referral strategy. By thinking about who your clients are and their motivations, you'll start empathising with what they are looking for from you. You'll understand why they buy from you and shape your brand messaging to fit. Even if the day-to-day work you do does not change depending on your client's persona, the messaging, marketing strategy and referral strategy will be dramatically different. Coke Zero is not that different to Diet Coke, men's moisturiser is similar to women's. But the branding varies wildly depending on whether the product is aimed at a man or a woman.

Client personas point you in the direction of where they hang out and where you reach them. If you can't reach your target clients, they are not much use. If you know that your typical client persona is a medical professional, go to events aimed at doctors and nurses. Join online forums for doctors, find what social media they use. Make your personas more accurate as you interact with their real-world counterparts. If your message resonates with doctors more than nurses, either tweak the message until it resonates with nurses too or try focusing just on doctors.

Profitable client personas are likely to emerge over time from your existing business. Where you notice that you are picking up a certain type of client, consider why that is and whether there are enough of that client type to build a sustainable niche. Experiment with your messaging, lean into it and you may find yourself as the go-to service provider with that group.

Referrer personas

To build a referrer persona, the starting point is the ideal client persona. Imagine that you are an accountant and have established that one of your client personas is a car salesperson in Chicago, the next step is to think about who might know car salespeople in your area and be able to introduce you to them. There is no right answer here; the point is to experiment to find which people refer you the best work. In this case, you could start with managers of car dealerships and garages.

If you find that this referrer persona provides you with great referrals, find more people in this category and tailor your referral strategy around them. If no referrals are forthcoming, try another referrer persona and keep going until you find one that consistently sends you high-quality referrals.

Value proposition

Your value proposition is the reason your clients choose you. It does not mean the features of your service, but the outcome you help your clients achieve in the context of the costs and differences between you and your competitors. As with your client and referrer personas, knowing your value proposition will ensure your message is clear and reaches the right clients and referrers.

We will look at building your value proposition for clients and your value proposition for referrers, which are subtly different. Get them right and referrers will find you the easiest person to send work. Do it wrong and referrers will be confused about what you do and you will miss out on work.

It's worth taking a moment to consider what we mean by value itself. It does not mean price. Instead, think of it as follows:

$$Value = benefits - costs$$

Benefits should be thought of as both rational and emotional; they do not mean features of your service. For example, the rational benefit of reading this book is that it will help you make money. The emotional value is that growing your business will make you feel successful, attractive and safe. We have evolved to want things that help us to survive and reproduce, so any value that any business provides will, however remotely, be about survival or sex. It does not mean that this book will help you meet the partner of your dreams.

On the other side of the ledger, costs are more than the financial cost of a service. They also include non-financial considerations like time, opportunity cost, risk, social stigma, reputation and physical pain. The costs of hiring a physical trainer might include the fee, the time for the sessions, aches and tiredness. If the physical trainer is able to reduce the non-financial costs, it follows that they will be able to maintain a higher financial cost and charge the client a higher fee. When figuring out your value proposition, identify these hidden costs and how to reduce them before you consider lowering your fees.

Your value does not exist in a vacuum: there are alternatives or competitors to your service. Service providers are usually operating in crowded markets, which are referred to as red oceans because the number of competitors means that there is blood in the water. Blue oceans, on the other hand, are markets where a business creates an entirely new product without any competitors.

Whether in a blue ocean or red ocean, there will always be alternatives to your service, which include the client self-servicing or using an app or artificial intelligence. The benefits and the costs of your services will be constantly compared to these alternatives and your competitors. You therefore need to be confident as to what your value proposition is and how it sets you apart.

To determine your value proposition, write down the answers to these questions:

- Who are your client personas?

- What problems do your clients have?

- How does your solution or service solve that problem?

- What are the rational and emotional benefits of your service?

- What are the financial and non-financial costs of your service?

- What are the main competitors and alternatives?

- What makes you different from your competitors and the alternatives (your unique selling point or USP)?

For a corporate boutique law firm, the answers might be:

- **Client persona**: med-tech start-ups in London looking for angel investment.

- **Problem**: they need funding and lack even basic knowledge about how the process works.

- **Solution**: we help navigate this alien world so they can take on funding quickly from relevant angel investors with minimal risk.

- **Benefits**: they receive investment, feel successful and confident (and therefore attractive).

- **Costs:** legal fees are high, it takes time to engage with a new law firm; if they instruct the wrong one, it risks their business too.

- **Competitors**: other corporate law firms and legal tech start-ups.

- **USP**: we are lawyers who are entrepreneurs too, and experienced in the med-tech space.

In a red ocean, the hardest part of your value proposition is likely to be the last question. Much of the rest of the value proposition will be well established, but what distinguishes you from your competitors will be hard to figure out. To see how hard this is, just take a look at the average large law firm's website. They all claim to be different from the competition based on their expertise, communication and friendliness, and therefore fail to distinguish themselves at all.

There is a group of people who can solve this problem for you: your clients and referral partners. They have chosen you over other service providers so they like what you do. Ask them: why? Send them a survey, note down the words and phrases that they use and then use this when determining your value proposition. Spot the patterns and words that recur: the chances are that this will be your USP.

Your value proposition for referrers

A clear value proposition for your clients will make it easier to tell your referral partners what it is that you do. Your branding and messaging will be clear and the referrers will have you in mind as the go-to person for a particular situation. The value proposition for your referral partners is slightly different. They are not receiving any service from you directly and do not have the same problems as the potential client.

As you are providing a service for free to potential referral partners, you do not need to solve their core problems (otherwise they would be your client themselves). Your benefit to a referrer will only ever be a nice-to-have and will often be as simple as making them appear useful to their contacts: being seen as well connected is valuable in itself. As the referrer is not receiving a benefit for which they are willing to pay, the main cost to them is reputational risk. To take the example above of an accountant providing services for car salespeople in Chicago, their value proposition for referrers might look like this:

- **Referrer persona**: car showroom managers in Chicago looking to retain great salespeople and improve sales.

- **Problem**: retention. As car salespeople can work for anyone, building loyalty is hard.

- **Solution**: provide free accounting advice to salespeople to make them feel valued.

- **Benefits**: increase retention, profits and save recruitment time and fees. Become a popular manager, feel more successful and more attractive.

- **Costs**: the reputational risk if your service is bad.

- **Competitors**: other accounting firms, but most are not proactively offering know-how for free.

- **USP**: you're an accounting firm exclusively focused on car salespeople, so you know the specific issues in the industry.

As with the client value proposition, the best people to tell you your referrer value proposition are your existing referral partners. If you are trying to reach new referrer personas though, you will need to test your value proposition with each new persona.

Combining your referrer personas and value proposition

Let's say car showroom managers from Chicago are the first referrer persona that you are taking for a test drive. Consider their demographics, location, where they hang out and their problems you can help solve.

You want introductions to their contacts, the car salespeople, so what will you give them in return? Find out what they want by asking them. This helps you create your initial referrer value proposition which you need to test to see if it resonates. If they tell you that they struggle to retain the best car salespeople, offer them value that helps them do that. In this case, you could offer free guides and webinars for salespeople who work at the dealership or offer a drop-in session to answer their accounting queries. Use the bullet points above and your initial email to car showroom managers almost writes itself: you have clearly set out your value from the referrer's point of view, not your own. If they reply saying they are not interested, politely ask why and if there is anything else that might be useful for them and their contacts.

If they like the value proposition, they will be happy to make the introductions to the car salespeople they know. The key is that you offer something of value to both the ideal referrer and the ideal client that directly relates to your expertise and is free for both.

If you obtain referrals from this new referrer persona, it is not the end of the story. You need to measure whether introductions actually convert into paying clients and if they don't you need to figure out why. Throughout this chapter we have treated the building of personas and value propositions as experiments. To determine the results of these experiments and analyse the journey from referral to client, we need to collect the right data and use simple metrics to help us analyse them, which is the subject of the next chapter.

Careful use of referral fees can be a great revenue stream

Kevin Smith, Boom & Partners

Used correctly, referral fees have an important place in the referral strategy. At their simplest, referral fees are a sum paid by the recipient of a referral to the person making the referral. They are usually calculated as a percentage of the fees paid by the client for that project or in the first one or two years following the introduction.

Kevin Smith, founder of award-winning business consultancy, Boom & Partners, is no stranger to collaborating with businesses, government agencies and charities around the world. He uses referral fees, but cautiously. He only takes on work that fits firmly within his expertise and brand, so at networking events his commonest phrase is, 'we are not the best person to help, but I know someone who is'. He makes a lot of outbound referrals. Kevin says his starting position is the karma of business networking: the most profitable referral is one that brings you work in the future, not one that pays you a referral fee.

If you refer a client to someone who is no good, that will hurt your business and reputation (which is crucial for professionals and easy to lose) far more than anything you might gain from a small referral fee. So when making a referral, the client's needs have to be foremost in your mind. Whether there is referral fee is irrelevant.

Only when he already has a good relationship with a referral partner whom he trusts to provide a good service to his clients is he happy to pay (or be paid) a referral fee. The arrangement is relaxed and agreed over email. As it is what Kevin calls a nice to have, it is not necessary to formally document the arrangement. If the referral partner behaves badly, the loss of the referral fee is the least of his worries. In the interests of transparency and building trust with his clients, he tells the clients where a referral fee is being paid. As his clients are themselves founders, they understand the process, trust his judgment and appreciate the honesty.

Kevin concludes that the referral fee should never be the reason why you are making the referral and should not be your main income stream. His focus has always been on the quality, not the quantity, of his connections. A referral fee can be the sign of a healthy network, but Kevin cautions that if you make it your business model, you will watch the trust drain away and work dry up.

6

REFERRAL METRICS

Your referral strategy depends on personal connections, so like those connections, it will evolve. An approach that works for one referrer persona will not work for another and the value of referrers for your business will change over time. Data and metrics allow you to experiment, measure and respond to those changes. This chapter will look at what data you can collect and how it determines which efforts are best to pursue.

Experiments and failure

As service providers, we are experts in our fields. People come to us for answers. As someone highly qualified, experienced or both, we are comfortable being the source of authority. So when it comes to business development or marketing, it is difficult to admit that we do not know what we are talking about. Specialists cannot be experts in everything. That's why service providers exist in the first place. So the first step when building a referral strategy is to embrace your ignorance and be humble. Your lack of expertise is not a bad thing so long as you have an open mind and do not judge yourself harshly.

Your referral strategy will depend on your personality, business size, clients and value proposition. This book cannot hope to be prescriptive for every business. While we offer actionable advice, it is your interpretation as it applies to your business that matters. Rather than an instruction manual telling you what the perfect referral strategy is, we offer an approach based on data and metrics.

This approach involves experimentation, which is why a successful referral strategy depends on failure. Failure is uncomfortable for experts, but it is crucial to identifying your best referrers and increasing economic returns. For start-up founders and developers, this iterative approach based on experimentation is commonplace. Founders have all read Eric Reis's *The Lean Start-up* and developers are all familiar with the agile development methodology. For expert service providers, this approach is often alien and unnerving.

It should not be. It might require a psychological shift, but failure should not be feared. If you think of your failed attempts as results of experiments, then each failure is simply information. Conduct tests, collect data and use them to generate further insights and ideas to test. Use failure to refine your referral strategy. If each failure is a point on a graph, it is easier to deal with. Failure becomes something to embrace.

Fail with a purpose though. Gather the right data and analyse it properly, otherwise it's a strategic missed opportunity. The key metrics for a service business are the client lifetime value, conversion rate, cost of acquisition and churn rate. We'll take each of these in turn and consider how to use them to systematically grow your business and turn failure into success.

Client lifetime value

The client's lifetime value is calculated as follows:

$$\text{CLTV} = \text{the annual fees paid by a client} \times \text{the number of years as a client}$$

For service providers, your CLTV is likely to be high. Annual client fees can be significant and as the relationship is personal, you should expect clients to be loyal. It's what sets service providers apart from most goods businesses. You're providing a service for which you charge a premium.

The other side of this coin is that service businesses cannot scale in the same way as a goods business because, however many people you employ, you will always be limited by the number of hours in a day. You will therefore have fewer clients and each client will be more important to you than each customer is to a consumer goods manufacturer or grocer.

Calculating the estimated CLTV for your business is simple. Look at the fees paid per year for each client and how long they stick with you as their service provider. You will need to make some intelligent assumptions here, as some clients may stick with you for decades and you won't know this in advance. Ask AI to help inform the assumptions for client loyalty in your industry.

By sorting clients in a spreadsheet you can group them by client persona and see immediately which types of clients yield the highest fees over the long term. Taking on more of those types of clients will be better for your business. You will see that spending a little time and money to acquire such a client is profitable in the long run. By including in your spreadsheet details about how the client was acquired, you will see which clients are the results of referrals.

In our experience, the CLTV for clients gained through referrals tends to be higher than the CLTV for those obtained in any other way. Your referral partners know you. They know what you are good at, what you are like as a person and who you will gel with. They have a sense of what fees their contact will accept and what fees you charge. If your client personas and value proposition are clear, they can do this with a high degree of accuracy. So referrals should give you clients that fit, are loyal and generate money over the long term.

By measuring your CLTV you will be able to test if this is true for your business. If you notice that your referred clients are not yielding you a high CLTV, it's a missed opportunity. Consider why this is and what you can do to change it. If you notice that, as expected, referred clients do have a high CLTV, use this to motivate yourself to obtain more referrals and keep providing great service to your existing clients.

Conversion rate

Your conversion rate is the percentage of any given cohort which converts into paying clients. It is useful for comparing the efficiency of different strategies and identifying what blockages are stopping you at each stage of the conversion funnel from obtaining more clients. Identifying the conversion rate of your different marketing and business development efforts will help you put resources in the right place.

Typically, the conversion rate is used to measure the effectiveness of website conversion funnels, with the starting cohort being the number of visitors to your site over a period and ending with the number of paying clients acquired over the same period. By looking at the different stages of the user journey you can see where they lose interest or can't find the button they need to make an order. But you can also compare the conversion rate of other strategies. The conversion rate of networking events is likely to be far lower than the conversion rate of referrals received from your trusted referral partners. According to Shopify, the overall conversion rate for a website selling consumer goods is typically between 2.5 and 3 percent. For those selling professional services, it is only slightly higher.

The conversion rate can be broken down into different phases of the sales funnel: for example, from site visitors to people who book a call with you, and from people who book a call with you to those who ask for a quote and from there to paying client. If you break your sales funnel out in this way, you see where the blockages are and where you should be focusing your energies. If you have many site visitors but no one books a call with you, there is likely to be a problem with the content on your site or a technical issue. By spotting and improving the blockages at each stage, you improve the overall conversion rate.

For services businesses, the low conversion rate of websites is problematic. For an ecommerce business, a user who bounces from the site costs nothing in absolute terms. But for a services business, an unqualified and unlikely prospect might need to speak to you before deciding not to instruct you, which wastes time you do not have. Where clients do not know you, they are likely to be shopping around for a good price and will think nothing of ghosting you. A low conversion rate at this stage costs service businesses time and money.

Client acquisition cost

Your CAC is the cost of acquiring each new client. If you use paid advertising, it is relatively easy to calculate: simply divide your total advertising spend in a period by the number of clients you acquire as a result of that spend. It is more complicated for service providers as clients do not sign up because of a Google ad alone.

One client takes time to land, including initial emails, initial call, quote, due diligence and entering into a potentially bespoke client contract. If you are a sole practitioner and do not outsource this process, the CAC is your theoretical hourly rate multiplied by the time it takes to land clients, including time spent on prospects who do not convert. CAC for service businesses is therefore potentially huge and is only justified because the CLTV of the client is high.

The combination of a high CAC and low conversion rate is a pernicious combination. Thinking that many quotes will be unsuccessful, service providers can be tempted not to invest time in accurate quoting, so the final invoice may bear little resemblance to the initial estimate. Where work is done on a fixed fee, it is the service provider who loses out. Either way, client and provider feel the process is not a good one. It makes for a stressful life.

Referrals, on the other hand, usually have a high CLTV, high conversion rate and high CAC. They are the goose that lays the golden egg but they require time and work to land. Incremental improvements in these metrics as applied to referrals therefore have a disproportionate effect on your business's fortunes (and your cortisol levels).

Churn rate or retention rate

The churn rate is the number of clients lost each year, expressed as a percentage of the total number of clients. You can analyse different cohorts too, such as different client personas. The churn rate tells you, bluntly, how good you are at your job. The retention rate is the opposite of the churn rate.

Churn rate = the clients who leave you in a period expressed as a percentage

Given the high CLTV and high CAC for service provider clients, prioritise the retention of an existing client over the acquisition of a new one. An additional year in the lifetime of a client relationship is a lucrative gain. For example, if the CAC for a client is £200 and average annual fees are £1000, each additional year for an existing client is worth £1000 whereas the first year of a new client is worth £800. Reducing the churn rate is not entirely free, but costs are less than the CAC, because the CAC takes into account all the time and money spent on prospects who never convert into clients.

The gains add up. As Sean Ellis and Morgan Brown report in their seminal book, *Hacking Growth*, researchers have discovered that 'a 5 percent increase in retention leads to an increase in profits of between 25 and 95 percent, because just small gains in retention lead to compounding revenue growth the longer customers stick around'. Einstein described compound interest as the eighth wonder of the world. For service businesses, that title goes to your churn rate.

For service providers whose clients tend to need one-off work rather than regular work over the course of a year or several years, your churn rate will appear much higher. Do not worry: a client who does not give you any work in a year has not necessarily churned. Deal with this in calculating your average annual fee, so that a client who pays you £3000 once every three years has an annual average fee of £1000.

A referred client should churn less than clients who come you by other means. If this turns out not to be true for your business, then you have an issue which needs fixing. Of all the suggestions in this book, reducing your churn rate will have the surest impact on your business's success.

Referrer metrics

Now let's use these metrics to find the best referrers. They should be pampered and nurtured, because they drive the growth of your business. These are your stars.

The best referrer is one who regularly introduces clients to you which have a high CLTV, high conversion rate, low CAC and low churn rate. Unfortunately, you will not have enough data to calculate these figures reliably individually for each referrer. Even the best referrers won't introduce more than a few clients to you each year. To make use of metrics in your referral strategy, take a step back and apply them to referrer personas rather than individual referrers. At this level you have more meaningful data and can make comparisons and measure changes over time. In addition to the data and metrics above, the key referrer persona metrics are:

- RP referrals: the number of paying clients received by referrals per year per referrer persona.

- RP billings: the fees billed by clients per year per referrer persona that introduced them.

Referrer personas with a high RP referral number, who send you many referrals who convert into clients are worth keeping on side. RP billings show you the monetary value of your relationships with different referrer personas.

The problem with calculating referral metrics at the persona level in this way is that they will be skewed by the number of referrers in each category. If you know many more accountants than hair stylists, it is likely their referral number and referral billings will be higher. To counter this effect, identify the number of referrers you know who fall into each persona category to obtain the average RP referral number and average RP billings for each referrer persona. These averages then allow a direct comparison between different referrer personas.

As these metrics are annual, they allow you to track the effectiveness of your referrer personas over time. If you notice that your best referrer types are sending you fewer referrals than before or the fees generated are lower, further investigation is necessary. It may be that they have forgotten about your services. It is an invitation to reach out to your referrers and listen to their feedback.

Referral fees

Much of this book has focused on how to use inbound referrals to obtain more clients. Some businesses will be able to make money from outbound referrals – referrals you make to other people – through referral fees. As we saw with Kevin Smith's case study, referral fees allow businesses to monetise the introductions they make directly. They usually involve a percentage commission being paid to the referrer by the service provider.

If you find yourself frequently introducing clients to other people, measure these relationships in the same way as your inbound referral relationships. There is little harm in discussing referral fees with partners you already trust. Many businesses are happy to pay referral fees, particularly if you have already proven yourself as a good referrer. If you are reticent about asking directly, say: 'it seems that you value the referrals you receive from me. Shall we make it more long term?' Be silent, and let them propose the referral fee themselves.

Referral fees constitute a great additional income stream that involve little work on your part. Amplify this revenue stream by analysing the sort of work you tend to refer out, and where it comes from. Identify who asks you for referrals, and who you refer them to. This will allow you to spot more opportunities at events and between your contacts and link the relevant people together.

The other way to look at referral fees is from the point of view of the business that is receiving the introduction. Businesses can set up referral programmes, by which they let it be known that anyone who refers them work will receive a percentage fee in return. We discuss this with the founders of introstars, Mike Adams, later in this book. Alternatively, where the referrer is a client, the business seeking inbound referrals can also discount the fees they would otherwise charge to the referrer.

It's important to note here that, as Kevin Smith highlights, a referral fee should never be the reason for making an introduction. Only make referrals to service providers who you believe will do a great job. Your reputation can easily be lost if you make referrals to second rate partners. Bear in mind also that referral fees are inappropriate in some sectors such as government procurement, where a referral fee can look like a bribe.

With referral fees and referral schemes, the golden rule still applies: only make and receive referrals with people you know, like and trust.

The power of metrics

Metrics show you the value of playing the long game and should encourage you to keep going: the prize of clients with high CLTV, high conversion rate and low churn is worth it. By gathering the right information and calculating your referral metrics, you will identify your best referrer personas. Together these metrics also allow you to start modelling your referral strategy and testing your assumptions.

Assumptions are a fact of life, but in business they can land us in trouble. They are often mutually contradictory and don't stand up to reality. If you imagine you have a high conversion rate from attending a networking event, for example, you'll quickly see how unrealistic this is given your historic record. If you don't actually meet one new client per event, that dramatically changes the value of each event. Whatever your assumptions, data will allow you to correct them and turn them into facts or falsehoods, which are much surer ground on which to build a business.

But data is by its nature impersonal and, as a service business, you should play to your strengths, which is the connection you have with your clients and referrers. As a service provider, your analysis must be more qualitative than quantitative and metrics should fit within your holistic, client-centred approach.

Treat your clients to meet their contacts

Thad Cox, Creative Heist

With a little creativity, you can get your existing clients to do a lot of your business growth work for you. Thad Cox, founder of Creative Heist, a marketing and media services company, tells of a technique he has learnt through many years of working with professional businesses and artists.

Your clients are your best referrers, especially after you have just completed a project for them. Your brilliance is fresh in their memory. Thad says that this is the best time to ask them for referrals. But many professionals hate doing that, so rather than asking directly, he recommends another approach.

After the project has completed, invite your client for dinner to say thank you for the work. That is great practice for referrals anyway, as it shows some love to your client and reduces churn. But the genius of Thad's approach is to ask the client to invite four or five of their contacts who might also benefit from his services. Clients love doing this, because it allows them to add value to their contacts too. Who doesn't love a free dinner and great introductions to people with similar challenges and opportunities?

At the dinner, don't sell to them, but try to understand any problems they have. You're trying to find an excuse to keep in touch after the dinner. If you can help them directly, great. But if instead you refer them to someone else, that's good too. Enter their details into your CRM, follow up with a call or email, responding to the pain point identified at the dinner, and diarise to follow up with them again. They are in your system and you are on their radar as the highly recommended and well-connected expert.

You're paying for dinner, so this strategy isn't free. But Thad says it is worth it. He finds that the conversion rate from these dinners is about 50 percent. You're not selling, you're just getting to know the client and showing your generosity. Your existing client has done the hard work, by identifying your potential clients and singing your praises. Even in the worst case and you get no new work, you have made an existing client happy. And you never know, you might get invited back for dinner.

7

STRATEGIC RELATIONSHIPS

Data and metrics provide a great overview of the state of your referrals, but collaboration depends on the strength of your relationships. Service businesses rarely have enough data to make decisions based purely on the numbers, but this is an opportunity for service businesses, rather than a weakness. As a service provider your relationships are key, and the process of gathering qualitative information and getting to know people is part of the relationship-building process.

Having analysed your data and identified your best referrer personas, examine what they have in common and listen to them to find out what you can do better. They will give you clues as to what you are doing right and where other great referrers might come from in the future. They are also the people you want to remember and rate you. Happily, the best insights come from the relationships on which you most want to build. The information-gathering and relationship-building conversations reinforce each other.

Identifying strategic relationships

These conversations are the most valuable you will have for another reason too. Thad Cox's approach of taking clients for dinner shows that information gathering and relationship building put you in a good place to ask for more referrals. Given the power of these conversations, do not waste your time gathering opinions from prospects who are unlikely to become clients or referrers. You have limited time, so only pick the low-hanging fruit. Focus on your best referrers and build strategic relationships.

The metrics will point you to those referrers who refer high-quality work. Looking at your data, you will notice that your best referrers are:

- **Your clients**: if you are doing a decent job, your existing clients should be your best referrers. Thad Cox picked up on this insight when organising his dinners. Clients know you and what services you provide.

- **Your friends**: even if they lack knowledge of your business, their enthusiasm for you as a person makes up for it. But if you have been in practice for a while, many of your friends will work in your sector too.

- **Your colleagues**: if you work in a large company, hopefully some of your best referrers are colleagues in other departments.

You might notice some trends in your data: maybe your best referrer personas are independent financial advisers. Maybe they are old school friends or members of your running club. If they are IFAs consider that other IFAs might also be a great referrer persona. Then find events with IFAs to attend and build relationships with more of them.

When describing your services to these new contacts, use the language you wrote down earlier from your conversations with IFAs when you were building your referrer value proposition. Show that you know what IFAs want in a referral partner. In this way you are building your referral network efficiently, using data, metrics and conversations.

Keep up this behaviour as a habit. It is not a one-off. Keep attending events, keep noting down who is giving you referrals. You will see patterns emerging that will inform your strategy. The more you do this, the more you will learn about who your best referrers are and what they respond to.

Consider repeat work as a referral

It is not technically a referral when an existing client gives you repeat work, but it is useful to put it in this category to stop you from taking your clients for granted. Repeat work from the same client is therefore the easiest referral to receive and should be prioritised. Your focus should be to reduce your churn rate to increase the value of each client.

As such, your churn rate is your key dashboard metric to know off by heart. Use the number to motivate yourself and track it over time. Reduce this number and, to some extent, the rest will follow.

Provide a high-quality service and combine it with excellent communication skills, clarity on fees and a relentless focus on your client's priorities, and they will not only not churn, they will also want to refer you to their contacts. A focus on the churn rate therefore increases the referral rate too.

Relentlessly focus on your best referrers

Once you have identified your best referrers, give them the red-carpet treatment and seek to build bonds of deep, affective trust. Like Thad Cox, take your clients and top referrers for drinks, dinners, coffees and any other form of informal contact that is appropriate for the relationship. Client entertainment is a great way of getting to know your clients and referral partners informally, which allows you to bond over shared interests. Do this in a genuine way and it won't feel like work. If golf really is a passion you share with a client, then invite them for a round. If you prefer musical theatre, find those of your clients who do too and seek out the drama. The more unusual the shared interest, the more memorable it (and you) will be.

Treat your best referrers like human beings, not prospects or targets. Cynicism will be discovered and you will lose any affective trust that you have built up between you. You should be working with people you like, so you should genuinely want to see these referrers. Occasionally arrange to see them just because you want to spend time with them. Regularly ask your key referrers for help. Whether it's advice on their area of expertise or emotional support, asking for help is a great way to build know, like and trust. It makes people feel trusted and so more likely to trust you. You will gain valuable advice and assistance. Be generous in offering advice and support in return. This approach might not be efficient, but by making your work life enjoyable, it is sustainable. As we are talking about your best referrers, it is likely to be efficient in the long run too.

As well as getting to know, like and trust each other, your aim is to ask some specific questions. Ask the referrer why they refer work to you. What is it that they see in you? Ask them how they describe your services to other people. Is there any constructive feedback they can share? This provides you with valuable information and also makes them feel important and listened to. Write their answers down, noting the specific words they use. Use this for your marketing later. If they have misunderstood the service you offer, update them and make a note to clarify your messaging.

Add them to your list for greetings for seasonal and religious festivals. To be consistent, send out seasons' greetings for the main religious and cultural groups. It is simple but will distinguish you from those who only pay attention to their own culture. You avoid having to send generic season's greetings and instead can wish people a Happy Christmas, Eid Mubarak or Happy Pride. You should feel able to send these messages to everyone, but if you go one step further and take note of which is relevant to each contact, they will feel seen, which is a great way to be liked, trusted and remembered.

Do not underestimate the power of gifts. So rare are gifts in business life, that they do not need to be personalised or expensive to be effective. Indeed, if you have a go-to gift which is somehow linked to your service, this can reinforce your brand. One law firm on the Adviserly network sends out beers to referrers, but the beer is given a name like First Draft, to make the recipient smile and remember that it was their lawyer who sent it to them. Send out these gifts at the relevant season or as a thank you for a referral. A little creativity goes a long way to help them remember you when they or their contacts are looking for an expert.

At the end of each quarter or year, make a note of clients you think have churned or referrers who have stopped referring work and contact them. The idea of a call might be uncomfortable, but the aim is to reconnect and, if there is a reason for the change in behaviour, to ask for feedback. The feedback of a client or contact who used to rate you highly but no longer does will provide actionable insights to improve your business. You might not like it but do it if you are serious about growing your business. The simple act of reaching out is so unusual that it may rekindle the relationship.

Seek internal client referrals

Large enterprise clients that have many internal departments are ripe for internal referrals. If you are an employment lawyer who acted on a dispute for the sales team, the easiest referral opportunity is to act for other teams in the same company. For these large clients, identify the internal referral opportunities. Which other departments should you be speaking to? Who makes the decisions?

When you are meeting your client as part of your regular client care process, ask them to invite any colleagues who might also value your services. Bring along any colleagues from your side who might also add value to the conversation. At no point should you make the hard sell. As a service provider rather than a salesperson, you are probably not inclined to do this anyway. Instead, ask the client open questions that do not invite a yes or no answer:

- How do you see business developing in the next year?

- What are your plans for the department?

- Which teams do you work closely with?

- What are the main blockers to growth?

- How can we best support you?

- Do you see other teams that might benefit from our services?

We recommend that you don't say:

- 'Who else should we be talking to?' This makes it sound like they're not important.

- 'What issues do your colleagues need help with?' They won't know.

- 'Who is stopping us from receiving the work?' This comes across a bit passive aggressive.

Keep your questions open during these conversations. Demonstrate your expertise by using statements that start with 'it seems that' and invite them to confirm or contradict you. 'It seems that your intellectual property is a strategic business asset for you' will elicit a more expansive response than 'do you have problems with your IP?' Try it and see how they open up and talk about their problems.

You are looking for information that can guide you through their organisation. Then follow up with specific information by email or phone responding to their queries or which pre-empt issues you have seen in similar clients. Refer back to the conversation and say, 'given what you said about the challenges of your business, your colleague in the sales team may also find this useful'. By giving them useful information for their colleagues, you are helping them add to their own social capital within the business. It is a powerful motivator if someone wants to impress a boss or colleague. You will receive an introduction not because you are asking for work, but because you provide specific, useful information.

If you share a passion with your referral partner, organise a group to attend a show or a match. Ask them to choose a small number of their colleagues to invite. You're making them popular and they will be grateful for the additional social capital within their company. Like a private members' club, keep it to a select group to add a sense of exclusivity and make yourself a desirable contact to know. You'll bond faster over shared interests and find your network within the client growing fast.

Keep tabs on alumni

Your best referrers will change jobs. This can represent a loss to your business if it means that works dries up from a previously reliable client. The upside is that opportunities are seeded in new potential clients. If a reliable referrer moves to a different business, keep in touch with them. Organise a coffee to see how they are getting on in their new role. They will be finding their feet and looking to impress their new colleagues, so help them do that.

People move jobs but rarely move industries, so their new company is likely to need your services too. Their new berth may however already have a service provider who does what you do and will not be willing to change. Your job is to investigate how loved the existing service provider is and what their shortcomings are. Actively poaching clients is exhausting and can dent your reputation if it is done brazenly. Instead, make sure the relevant people at the company know what you do, so you are first in line when they look for a replacement or supplemental provider.

In the same way as you would for a referrer at an existing client, invite them and their colleagues to events based around your shared interests, provide information that is useful for them and their colleagues, and seek internal client referrals. By being thoughtful during a time of vulnerability, you will strengthen your personal bond and find yourself with an advocate in a new potential client. Even if the referrer's new employer never refers you any work, you will have created great new contacts who may leave and seed your interests in yet more potential clients.

Ask for referrals from your best referrers

Ask your referrers and clients for referrals directly. Just come out and say it. Remember how busy you are? We want only to take the easiest step and the easiest way to get something is to ask for it. It can feel uncomfortable when you do it at first, so here's how to approach it.

We will assume you have established your credentials as someone useful, who genuinely listens to your client's views, so you have earned the right to contact them spontaneously. Call or message them with news that they may not have seen but which is useful to their business. 'I'm just calling to highlight this change to the tax deadline' is a call they will be grateful for. Contact them to ask their opinion in their area of expertise as nothing builds trust in you like your trust in them. They will look forward to speaking with you. Outside these spontaneous calls, you should be holding regular catch ups with your clients too.

At the end of these conversations, use this killer statement: 'We have capacity to take on one more client at the moment. Who do you know that might benefit from talking to us?' This statement looks contrived but it works. Change it to suit your circumstances and personality but there are two key elements:

- By emphasising that you have capacity for one more client, you show that you are busy, in demand and that your high-quality services are scarce. It also contains the extent of your request. You are not looking for ten introductions, you are looking for one.

- Ask 'who do you know?' (you are looking for a name), not 'do you know anyone who?' (it's easy to say no to a yes/no question).

If they can't think of anyone immediately, they will leave the conversation with the question hanging in their minds. Alternatively, they may have someone to introduce you to immediately, in which case you have won the easiest warm introduction of your life. Before the conversation ends, give them a specific task, which is to send you the person's name and contact information or LinkedIn profile. You want to reduce the amount of work they have to do, so don't ask for an introduction. An introductory email can take a surprising amount of time to write. When they give you their contact's details, write to the contact and copy in the client and explain the connection. For almost no effort, your client gains social capital in this situation: they have connected two people who are useful to each other.

By spending time talking to your client and exploring their problems, they will be well disposed to you. The human instinct to reciprocate will mean that they want to do something for you. Your value to them will rise and they are less likely to churn. So you please the client, reduce your churn rate, extend the client's CLTV and gain a warm lead to another high-value client.

Convert referral partners into strategic partners

The best referrers should become strategic partners in your business. With these partners, whether inside an organisational structure or between independent businesses, if they thrive, you thrive and vice versa. These are the most powerful referral relationships but you can only have so many so you will need to be judicious. Referral metrics will provide clues to who might be the best strategic partner, but you need qualitative information too. Discuss vision and strategic objectives with all your best referral partners and you will find those who most closely align with your business.

Your strongest referral relationships will be with those who share your motivations. As Simon Sinek says in *Start with Why*: 'personal recommendations go a long way. We trust the judgement of others. It's part of the fabric of strong cultures. But we don't trust the judgement of just anyone. We are more likely to trust those who share our values and beliefs.'

Once you have found a strategic partner, try hosting events together, approaching clients together and branding your work together. The more closely you work, the more important it is to have your legal documentation in order (and by now you should know where you can come to for legal advice).

Conclusion

Your personal relationships are the keystone of your referral strategy. The goal of this chapter has been to help you increase the number of clients introduced from your best referrers, find more of them and build strategic relationships. Focus on those best referrers, listen, learn and make it easy for them to make introductions. Be useful to them by increasing their social capital within their business or network. Keep tabs on your clients' alumni and ask directly for referrals, whether internal or external. Turn your best referrers into strategic partners and thrive together.

Referrals have a better return than pay-per-click advertising

Alex Marinova, First Steps

Alex Marinova, founder of First Steps, a legal and business consultancy, tells a story that will be familiar to many professionals trying to build their own practice. After a year of running the business, she was sold the dream of outbound marketing. It's not unreasonable: if you spend money on Google, Facebook and LinkedIn ads, it is logical that, with a bit of experimentation, clients will eventually find you. It seems obvious because you know you are great, and you know that people often find their lawyers, accountants or any other professional (including marketing experts) through pay-per-click advertising.

But Alex's experience is instructive for many professional firms. In her first year of business, she spent thousands of pounds on PPC ads across various social media and Google. She received no new clients. There was some traffic to her website, but the enquiries were often outside her expertise or demanding a price point that was not economical for her. That's a return of 0 percent and an important lesson. Because meanwhile, her business was growing through referrals.

PPC advertising for professional businesses is wildly expensive, even if you get a return of more than 0 percent. There are many businesses competing for the same space online, so your ads have to be targeted to such a defined point (you're aiming for a needle in a haystack) that it's difficult to get the right wording to hit your ideal clients.

Alex's referral strategy, meanwhile, is free(ish) and yields regular new clients who pay her thousands of pounds in fees. Her favoured approach is to go to networking events and have a drink with potential clients. They get to know each other, get to trust each other and get to like each other. And she finds clients that are the right fit for her business, like a start-up researching a treatment for Alzheimer's, rather than the unfocused enquiries she receives through PPC advertising.

8

LEVERAGE MARKETING
TO DRIVE REFERRALS

Successful businesses follow the money. Given the primacy of referrals for service-business growth, the focus should be on building a referral strategy, of which marketing forms a vital but secondary component.

Marketing is a powerful tool, but to make the most of it you need to use it within the broader context of your referral strategy. Do not demand miracles from your marketing team, because, as we have seen, referrals take time but are hugely valuable. The role of marketing is to reinforce your personal brand and the brand of your firm by making it explicit who your clients are and what your value proposition is. Specifically, it must help build know, like and trust among your clients and referral partners. Marketing takes many forms, but this chapter will focus on:

- Websites

- Content marketing

- Newsletters

- Social media

- Reviews, case studies and testimonials

Not of all of these will be right for your personality or your sector and you will not have time to do it all. Experiment and find what yields the best results. Before we dive in though, it's important to put marketing in context and contain our expectations.

The limits of marketing-led growth

Referrals, business development and marketing are often conflated. Either referrals are seen as part of a marketing strategy or both referrals and marketing are seen within a broader category of business development. The growth potential for many services businesses is undermined by this lack of focus.

Most service businesses do not receive work directly from their marketing alone. Alex Marinova's story illustrates the limits of pay-per-click advertising for service businesses, while Jules Zeng told us that referrals are more powerful than search engine optimisation for her own SEO consultancy business. For any service, there are thousands of potential providers. There are so many brand consultants, builders and corporate lawyers that it is difficult for any one of them to stand out from the crowd. A potential client who googles 'UK lawyer to help sell my business' yields thousands of search results, but they all look the same. They are experienced, award winning, communicative, commercial and many have trust pilot reviews which apparently back this up.

But how does a client who only knows you from your website actually choose you? Experienced clients rely on their network to give them a referral. A client who makes an enquiry through your website will send enquiries to several service providers and compare responses. They are looking for answers to three questions:

- Do they like you?

- Are you a good communicator?

- Is it the best price?

What they are not judging is quality, because they cannot gauge it from your website or social media profile alone, or even from a quick conversation. A client only discovers if a service provider is any good when it is too late, sometimes only years later. Clients know this and have plenty of experience of being disappointed. So of these three factors, it often comes down to just price. If they don't know whether it's a good deal or a bad deal, they might as well opt for a cheap deal. All your expertise comes to nothing and price is everything.

No good service provider wants to find themselves in a price war. It takes time to quote for work and inexperienced clients who focus on price rather than value are not the clients that service providers want, as Alex Marinova found with enquiries that came through PPC advertising. Service is part art, part science, part conversation. There needs to be understanding and trust for the relationship to work. An ideal client is one with a high client lifetime value and a low churn rate, who does not make your life a misery with constant arguments about fees.

As websites and social media by themselves tend not to generate the best leads for service businesses, the tendency is to underinvest in them. You don't measure the conversion rate for your online presence so are never sure whether clients come to you from your website or through referrals. If you hire an agency to manage your marketing, you quickly become disillusioned by the questionable results and the cost. You don't commit and you blame your marketing team and underinvest. You never really give marketing a chance. It's a vicious cycle.

It is time to interrupt this cycle: you want clients to be referred to you, because they make for the best clients. Marketing is a bazooka in the armoury of your referral strategy, but it cannot perform miracles. Let's look at what marketing can and cannot do.

The role of marketing in the referral strategy

The development of a referral relationship relies on the degree to which you know, like and trust your partners. Marketing in your referral strategy should be working to those ends: either helping people know you and what your value proposition is, like you as a person, or trusting you to do a great job. If marketing is not serving one of these ends, it has no place in your referral strategy. To make this clear, we split marketing into three types: know marketing, trust marketing and like marketing.

Know marketing: to inform

Know marketing builds visibility and makes it easy for people to recommend you. It keeps you in the front of peoples' minds when someone asks for a referral. Be clear on what you do and who you want as clients. Relentlessly spread the word. You might become bored of this message, because you'll see it all the time. But your clients and referral partners do not. What is dull for you will be fresh for them.

Clients and referrers respond better when you show rather than tell. Give them examples, case studies and genuinely useful information for their business based on your expertise. Inform your clients and referrers how you work, the steps in your onboarding process and, if you have a referral programme, what it looks like.

Like marketing: to connect

As a species geared towards survival, we rely on simple rules of thumb, or heuristics, to make quick decisions which enable us to survive in a competitive world. In Daniel Kahneman's celebrated book, *Thinking Fast and Slow*, he explains how we have evolved to make fast decisions without involving our slow, deliberative mind. We have evolved to judge a book by its cover.

It is not just your appearance, though that is important; it's about how you come across. Clients want someone to be likeable and approachable. They want to be able to ask you questions and not feel like an idiot. Make it clear they can sit down and talk to you. Referrers do not want to refer people to someone who comes across as unpleasant.

Trust marketing: to reassure

Remember that the mantra of the successful referrer is trust, but verify. No one wants to refer their family, friends or colleagues to a bad service provider. The referrer or client already thinks you are good, that's why they have come to your website. They check you out online to verify that opinion. Your online presence therefore needs to do no harm: do not give them reasons not to trust you.

When a referrer makes a referral to you, they are risking their reputation. Your priority is to lower that risk as much as possible. Show attention to detail. Think of it like you would a CV. A single typo or bad photo can be fatal, because it shows a lack of thoroughness. Show you have the relevant qualifications, experience and resources to take on the work.

Marketing that is designed to encourage trust does not need to make you stand out, and in some ways, it should do the opposite. It is designed to make you fit in with the pack. The phrase 'no one ever got fired for hiring IBM' is such a business cliché because clients don't want to gamble their careers on hiring a service provider who is outside the norm. Professionals who place a premium on trust, like lawyers, therefore tend to have websites that all look the same. It is a great skill to combine reassuring trust marketing while making your value proposition and unique selling point clear.

Building a referral-friendly website

Your website is the foundation of your know, like and trust marketing, so let's look at the key elements of a website in the context of your referral strategy.

Referrers by definition are savvier than the prospects they are referring to you. They will be more familiar with what a good website looks like than the average client. Accountants are familiar with professional websites and hair stylists are used to websites in the cosmetics industry. For your referral strategy, your website does not just need to impress the uninformed, it needs to impress other experts too.

Your profile photo

A good profile photograph is entry level like-and-trust marketing. A grainy photo, bad lighting or one that is unflattering will turn people away. Whether they want to flirt with you or work with you, a bad photo will stop them. It is the first impression. Referral partners want someone who is likeable, relatable and cares about quality. A bad photo makes you look sloppy at best and murderous at worst.

The founders of Airbnb discovered that professional photos of listed apartments were the key to encouraging users to book, as no one wanted to stay at a place if the photos were bad. They sent photographers to visit the early site listings and turned a struggling start-up into the global giant we know today. Or consider the importance of photos on dating apps, which provide detailed advice to make you look your best. Ensure the style of photograph is the same across your organisation. It will show consistency and make it clear you are a coherent team that works together. Whether it's on your website, LinkedIn or Tinder, your face matters. Use it well.

Your shop window

Your website has a crucial role in trust marketing. After they meet you or are referred to you, people will check your website. A good website might not drive much work to your business, but it will stop you losing it.

Your site may not need a full revamp, but so many sites get the basics wrong. What does a user see when searching your firm on Google? When on your site, what logo is showing in the browser's address bar? (This is called the favicon and it should never be the Wordpress logo.)

Do not use stock images. They say that you have not invested any time or money on your website, because no designer worth their salt would let these images near it.

A sloppy website could well indicate sloppy work. It suggests you are not commercial and you are not interested in the business side of your work, which raises the question: why on earth would you be interested in the business of your clients?

Your notice board

Your website is your best opportunity to inform, so it is the foundation of your know marketing. It explains who you are and what clients you work with. By looking at your homepage, clients and referral partners should have no doubt that you are qualified to do the work they need you to do. Any doubt here makes receiving the referral less likely, as no one wants to waste their time asking if the work is in your skillset.

The images and text on your site should speak directly to those messages. They should target your clients, even including images of your target clients, showing who your existing clients are and telling their stories.

Referral programmes and pages

If your business primarily grows by referrals, have a page on your website setting out the importance of referrals to you and how you roll out the red carpet for your referral partners. Design the page to be shared by referrers with potential clients. If you aim to respond to referrals within a particular timeframe, set that out. Include a template referral email for your referral partners to use. It is great know-and-trust marketing and will make you stand out among potential referral partners.

If you have a referral scheme provide details including exclusive content, referral fees, discounts or free services for your referral partners. Be transparent so that your referrers know they are incentivised to make referrals, and so that there are no surprises down the line for clients.

Content marketing for referrals

High-quality content, including written, video or audio, is great know-and-trust marketing. It is hard to measure the impact of content and you will rarely be certain it was this or that piece of content that brought you a new client. But your clients have a high CLTV, so even if your content is only one factor in landing a client or only directly lands one client a year, it is worth it. Be kind to your marketing team and let them help you produce regular quality content. The effect is cumulative, so keep going even if you don't see immediate returns.

Content contents

Whatever form it takes, write informative content and provide actionable information to the potential client. Do not worry that this appears to be giving away free advice. The content should start from the problem faced by the client. The reader or viewer is starting from an inexpert point of view and needs to be drawn into your expertise from a place they understand.

Your referral partners want to see that you are an expert who can solve the client's problem. The more valuable your content is, the more likely that the referrer will also share the content itself, so be sure to include a sharing link on each page for email sharing and for each of the major social media providers. All content must include a call to action, which is something the person is invited to do, such as filling in a form or subscribing to a newsletter.

Written content

Most people are not accomplished readers, which is why search engines rank web pages according to readability, as well as how well they respond to certain search terms. If your content is online, consider having an SEO expert review your text to ensure it is easy to read and responds to the current criteria for highly ranked searches. Even if you are not using SEO to draw people to your website, it is good practice because it means your content will be easy to read and focused on the user's concerns.

Video and audio content

Clients (and search engines, if you are worried about SEO) increasingly expect to see video and audio content, even in conservative industries. It covers all our know, like and trust objectives. A video of you talking to camera explaining how you will resolve a client's problem reminds people what you do but, more than written content, is also a great way for clients to gain a sense of who you are and whether they will like and trust you.

Service providers who are not digital natives often feel uncomfortable with video and audio. If you invest in it, you will set yourself apart, though this is likely to have diminishing returns as younger digital natives enter the workforce and take it for granted. At that stage, if you don't have video and audio content, you will be limiting your client base only to other non-digital natives.

Guest content

Your referral partners will share your content more if they feature in it. Invite your referral partners to guest write a blog or interview them on a webinar or podcast. Encourage them to tell your story and make more referrals to you. It gets you working together and building know, like and trust. They will become more familiar with what it is that you do.

Likewise, create free content for your best referrers. Content creation is difficult, so they will be grateful for your insights if it is relevant for their clients. Meanwhile, you are displaying services directly to your referral partners' website visitors. Assuming you have correctly identified your best referral partners, some of their clients will come directly to you, skipping the referral entirely.

Lead magnets

A lead magnet is content that is used to obtain contact details of potential leads. It can be a short ebook, a how-to guide, templates or anything else your clients might find useful. In the context of referrals, your lead magnets should be easily shareable, so that referral partners can send the lead magnet to others with just one or two clicks. It should be tailored to your value proposition for referrers and clients that we discussed above.

Newsletters

You never know when someone will come to your clients and contacts and ask: 'do you know anyone who can help with this problem?' It could be years after you last worked for a client, so there is a high chance they will have forgotten about you. It might be that the client is asking themselves this question and can't remember that you did a great job for them last time. Remember, treat repeat work as a referral. It's like your client's past self referring you to her future self.

Newsletters are classic know marketing, as you are reminding your referral partners what you do. Newsletters should be aimed squarely at your target client personas, including practical advice on solving problems and news on recent changes or upcoming deadlines. By giving away great content for free, straight to their inbox, you'll be the natural first person they come to when they, or someone else, needs your services again.

Have patience. The cost of producing a newsletter is low and their effect is accretive, but too many service providers give up after not receiving any work for their efforts. Newsletters are part of the referral long game and none the less valuable for that.

Social media marketing

Use social media to reach your target referral partners and remind them who you are and what you do. It is an upgraded version of the newsletter and, if you find the right channel for your business, can be more effective. The key is to find where your referral partners hang out online and focus your attentions there. Content needs to be tailored to the medium on which you are posting it, so do not try to copy and paste content across different platforms. If your referral partners are all lawyers, your content should be on LinkedIn. If your referral partners are journalists, try Threads or X.

In Jack Lineker's case study, we saw how interactions on social media can mimic interactions in a room full of referral partners. Someone posts a question on LinkedIn or Instagram asking if anyone can help with a particular project and a referral partner comments, tagging the service provider. It's the equivalent of someone introducing you at a party, but more efficient. We see this at Adviserly too: whether on LinkedIn or WhatsApp, lawyers ask for recommendations from their hive mind of experts.

Social media is difficult because each platform has different tech, communities and algorithms that change frequently. It is time-consuming as social media is interactive and requires responding to other users who comment on your posts. But we are increasingly online and commenting on posts is becoming as natural as talking at a party.

Reviews, case studies and testimonials

Case studies in which you tell your clients' stories from problem to resolution are great know marketing. It is better to show rather than tell because humans are obsessed by stories. Case studies show clients and referrers that you have the necessary expertise, how you approach a problem, and what they can expect in terms of solution and timeframe.

Testimonials and reviews are also useful trust marketing. Clients and referrers expect you to have happy clients as the bare minimum. Not having testimonials rings alarm bells. If your clients allow you to show their names on your website, it is great know marketing too, because it helps referrers and clients know that you work for businesses like them.

As reviews, case studies and testimonials are standalone content, they are easy to share on social media and in your newsletters. Integrate review, testimonial and case study requests into your client onboarding and exit processes to generate a constant flow of fresh content.

The referral bazooka

Marketing is a powerful part of your referral strategy. Focus on building know, like and trust with your referrer and client personas and you will remind them that you exist as well as what you do, while also proving your expertise, verifying your credentials and showing that you are likeable and trustworthy. There is fun to be had in finding the medium that works best for you, given your strengths and weaknesses and the industry in which you operate.

Doing marketing well can make you a referral partner of choice. If you ignore it, prepare to be ignored.

Attend events to gain referrals, but don't forget to follow up

Jimmy Vestbirk, Legal Geek

Networking events are one of the best places to generate referrals, but not necessarily in the way people think. Jimmy Vestbirk is the founder of events company, Legal Geek, which has turned traditional boring legal networking on its head.

In 2015 Jimmy was looking to found a legal tech start-up. He set up a group on the meet-up app to find other like-minded people, what he calls a 'social prop'. But it was the meet-up group itself that would eventually grow, organically, into his main passion. He built it through referrals: people recommended their friends join the group, and everyone knew someone who could help make the events bigger and better.

From that small beginning, Jimmy built Legal Geek into one of the largest legal innovation communities in the world which hosts the largest law tech conference in Europe. As a regular attendee, I am struck by the contrast with other legal events, stuffy and charmless affairs, which do not encourage real human interactions. Jimmy says his proudest achievement is 'making the high five socially acceptable in the legal profession.' Those outside the legal world can only imagine the scale of that task.

Legal Geek is a relaxed event with short presentations, workshops, panels, food, drink and, most importantly, games. Jimmy explains that attendees are 'paying to access the mindset where people are willing to chat'. He sees his job as encouraging that mindset. At his early events, he created networking games to help break down social norms.

His first tip for making the most of the events is to enjoy them. If you give off a positive energy, you will attract people to you. He recommends some planning too: download the event app, search for the attendees that you want to meet, message them and arrange a time, or go to meet them at their stand if they have one. He says you should have a simple objective, like making five good connections. The biggest mistake he sees is the lack of follow-up: send emails, arrange for coffees, build on the relationship after the event.

As the founder of the event, he is naturally connected to a lot of people, and constantly making introductions between people who might be useful for each other. He says that generally people are receptive and grateful to be introduced, as they like to be asked for help. Don't be shy, he urges, when making introductions. And he should know, he's built a successful business out of it.

9

NETWORKING

In your referral strategy, marketing is the air war and networking is the ground war. Your air campaign reaches many people, but the land battle pits you face to face with your target clients and referrers. You will need to advance into the trenches and take ground one new connection at a time. Networking is laborious, but when it comes to referrals, in-person, meaningful connections are worth having. Most of your referral partners will come through a combination of networking and marketing.

In this chapter we use the word networking to mean both attending events and joining referral networks. Networking events, both virtual and in-person, offer unique opportunities to connect with potential clients, partners and peers. They are not just about exchanging virtual business cards; they are about making real-life, personal connections. When approached correctly, with what Jimmy Vestbirk calls the 'mindset where people are willing to chat', networking is an enjoyable and rewarding experience. It's about engaging with others, sharing your passions and finding common ground that can lead to lasting referral relationships. If networking is not fun, then you are doing it wrong.

It has to be efficient too; you are building a business after all. Inefficient networking is soul-destroying and time-wasting. After a while, you'll give up. One way to understand the potential of networking is through the concept of the networking funnel. At the top of the funnel are the large number of people you meet at events. As you move down the funnel, you collect and share contact details, leading to follow-up calls and meetings. These interactions help to build deeper connections, eventually transforming into friendships, partnerships and valuable referrals at the bottom of the funnel.

The aim is to make your networking funnel more efficient without losing sight of the idiosyncratic and random nature of human interactions. You might not get to high-fiving strangers like at Legal Geek, but should find yourself networking with a smile on your face. You want to reach the stage where your networking is fun and efficient, as well as fun because it is efficient. Successfully making valuable friendships and lucrative referral partnerships is a great feeling.

In this chapter, we will explore strategies for effectively using both online and in-person networking events, as well as referral networks. We will delve into different networking approaches depending on your personality and then provide practical tips for making meaningful connections, nurturing relationships and creating referral partnerships that deliver.

The networking funnel

We discussed earlier the concept of a conversion funnel and the metrics to use when measuring its success. The networking funnel works in the same way.

Networking takes time and often feels like it is time wasted, so keep the client lifetime value of the potential new client and referral partner in the front of your mind. When attending a networking event, you only need to obtain one client or referral partner to make the effort worthwhile. One referral of a £5000 piece of work could represent a x100 return on your event ticket price. And remember that one good referral partner is worth many future clients.

A networking funnel looks similar to a conversion funnel for a website:

- At the top of your networking funnel you have the attendees at an event. You do not want to speak to all of them: you won't get on well with everyone and most will not be useful to you and your business. But you will have to talk to a good number of people to find those who are. The more preparation you do before the event to identify your best potential clients and referrers, the more effective this sifting process will be.

- Amid the many short conversations at a day-long event, you only need to have ten good conversations with potential referrers.

- In these conversations, your objective is twofold: exchange contact details and have a reason for following up, such as to continue a discussion on an interesting topic or, even better, to make an introduction for them.

- Of the ten or so people you contact after the event, aim to have calls with five of them.

- Of those five, with some thoughtful nurturing, aim for one of them to become a high-quality referral partner.

For the remainder of this chapter we will keep the networking funnel at the forefront of the conversation.

Networking opportunities

Networking opportunities fall into three categories:

- Online networking events

- In-person networking events

- Referral networks

Aim to use all of these as part of a healthy referral strategy but find a balance which is right for you. Let's look at each in turn.

Online networking events

There are many networking events available online, including classes, webinars and virtual conferences. The primary goal may be educational, but they present networking opportunities with the speakers, as well as the other attendees. If there are break-out rooms and chat rooms, join them. Engage actively in any sessions for questions. If the event is worth going to, concentrate on it throughout. If isn't, don't go: attending an event while secretly filing your nails is not a productive use of the opportunity.

The aim is to identify as quickly as possible which of the attendees or speakers will make the best referral partner. After an online webinar, send a personalised message to each of the speakers to say you enjoyed the webinar and ask an open follow-up question to keep the conversation going. If you interacted with other attendees that might be good referral partners, message them to ask them their view of the topics discussed. Do not ask closed questions with yes/no answers. An hour-long webinar that yields one-long term referral partner is a bargain.

In-person networking events

Real world networking events come in all shapes and sizes. They include industry conferences, trade shows, workshops, local business events and policy forums. They come in the form of breakfasts, coffee mornings, lunches, dinners, roundtables, drinks, platform discussions, speeches, theatre trips, sports games, walks, runs and more. If it is possible to do it in person while fully clothed, someone has turned it into a networking event.

You have a surfeit of choice, so attend events that you enjoy. Networking should be fun, because then you'll keep doing it. Meeting strangers and discovering mutual passions, interests and humour is one of the great privileges of being human. So put your humanity first, find the events you enjoy going to and only then start thinking about referrals.

Referral networks

A referral network is a group of active referrers, willing and able to refer clients to each other. Given the high conversion rate and high CLTV of referred clients, these networks are gold mines for service businesses.

Some focus on particular industries or locations. Others are built around personal characteristics, such as gender or ethnicity. Your time is limited, so don't join them all. Experiment to find the best: you may discover that you have much better results with one group or prefer the people in another.

Referral networks usually offer a directory of other members, a chat group of some kind, such as Slack or WhatsApp, and regular online and in-person events. They come in many shapes and sizes:

- Chambers of commerce and local business clubs are great if you are looking for ad hoc work. They throw up good clients now and then and have nice in-person events close to where you work. There will be many different types of businesses in these groups. You will often be able to bring guests to the events, so take a client along and reward their loyalty. Given the somewhat random nature of membership of local clubs, you will need to be sure of the type of referral partner you want to talk to. Be targeted and say no to the more esoteric referrals that come your way.

- Sector networks focused around a particular industry or sector bring together people with different angles on the same problems. Imagine a chat group full of marketing experts, chief financial officers, developers and lawyers all working in education technology sector. Most members will not directly compete with you but they will have clients that you want to talk to, so they are great potential referral partners. The downside is that, depending on how exclusive the network is, members may already have a referral partner with your expertise from the same network, so might not be interested in talking to you.

- Professional networks, such as Adviserly, work because they bring together people with particular expertise who act in many sectors. At Adviserly, our members are all lawyers, but they act in different practice areas in different countries. They share a professional approach and education, so there is a high degree of mutual understanding. Lawyers specialise in a practice area so need to make referrals to other lawyers with different expertise. These groups are great for career progression though employers need to watch out for talent poaching. Make yourself interesting by challenging the received wisdom and group think.

- Networks based on personal characteristics, only open to certain categories of people, are great for those typically underrepresented in business. They increase participation in particular sectors by connecting mentors and mentees. These groups are particularly effective if focused around a sector, such as women in finance or LGBT tech start-ups. Personal connections can be especially strong when bound together by a common struggle against structural prejudice. While encouraging inclusion in the workplace, they are by definition exclusionary, so you'll want to be in other networking groups as well, to ensure your network is diverse.

- Government networking opportunities are provided by embassies and investment organisations. They want to attract inbound investment to their home country and assist businesses exporting to others. They organise standalone events as well as assisting other cross-border business forums. They can provide introductions and form the infrastructural spine around which great cross-border networks can be built, even if they are not themselves a network.

- Hobby clubs, such as sports or boardgames clubs, are great places to meet likeminded people where you can build strong bonds of affective trust, but they are less efficient for referrals. Use these purely for pleasure and treat any referrals as incidental bonuses. Business is important, but life is too short to always be on the clock. If you go somewhere to relax, relax. The exceptions are sports where exercise is incidental, such as golf. They are great ways to meet senior executives and financiers across many sectors and talk in person in a relaxed context. The downside is that you are forced to play golf.

Assemble your own supergroup

If you are struggling to find a network that is right for you, create your own group. Assemble non-competing businesses that share your target audience so that you cross-promote each other's services and make referrals.

As you are setting it up, ensure you like the people in the group and want to work with them. Make it an LGBT or women only group if that works for you. Set up a WhatsApp group, organise drinks and dinners among yourselves and get to know each other. Share the burden of organisation and keep things small and informal. Be generous with the advice you give and open about asking for what you need.

Fit the networking around your personality

Networking is personal. To leverage membership groups and networking events and build an efficient networking funnel, make a plan based on your personality. If you are anxious in large groups, go for smaller events and online networking. Your personality type will inform what events you go to and also how you behave at those events.

Do not judge people with different personality types to you: introverts are not weak or shy and extroverts are not loud and imposing. Be patient and tolerant. Prepare to be surprised by people you might not expect to like, but equally don't waste time with people you really don't get on with.

How to translate networking into referrals

To ensure networking is an effective part of your referral strategy:

- Identify the right events

- Prepare

- Behave well

- Have fun

- Provide value

- Ask for referrals

- Follow up

Identify the right events

The first mistake that people make with networking events is going to the wrong ones. They waste time with people who will not instruct them or refer them work. For example, at events promoted as an opportunity for start-ups to pitch to investors, you find many start-ups but few investors. At events designed for start-ups, you will find lawyers, accountants, business advisers and only the occasional founder. Why is this?

People go to events, at some level, to sell. Straight men and women go clubbing to meet the opposite sex and, in effect, sell themselves, though the currency they are looking for in return is not money. A club night that highlights the number of attractive straight women who attend is designed to attract straight men. There is a lesson here for our referral strategy.

Let's acknowledge that events organisers have a difficult job. They are curating a one-off multi-sided marketplace and need good taste in venue, food and drink. If an event bills itself to a tech start-up founder as an opportunity to meet investors, you'd hope that those investors are receiving messages that invite them to meet the next unicorn.

But there are always more sellers than buyers at events, putting buyers in a position of considerable power. In this case, founders are selling shares and investors are buying them, putting the investor in control. The events to attend are therefore those where your clients or referrers will be the sellers. There will be more of them and you will be competing against fewer people for their attention.

Let's say you are an accountant who has identified that tech start-ups are your best referral partners. You know your target referrer wants to sell shares to investors, so go to events billed as investor events. Few accountants will think they need to pitch to investors, not realising that this is fertile ground to find this type of referral partner. Chances are, you'll be one of only a few accountants there. At worst, you will learn about the investment concerns of start-ups, which you then use in conversation the next time you meet a founder. At best, you meet great referral partners there and then.

So build this in to your referral strategy: attend events where your targets are the sellers and you will always be in the right room.

Prepare for your events

Your event preparation should consist of:

- Identifying your referrer personas, based on your referral metrics and the analysis of your data.

- Reviewing the list of attendees to see who in these categories is attending and identifying those you want to talk to. Reach out to them on the conference app, if there is one, or connect with them in advance on LinkedIn to say you are going to the same event and you are looking forward to meeting them. It will make it easier to speak to them in-person.

- Deciding what value you will offer your referral partners. It could be an invitation to another event, a free consultation for them or their clients or content tailored specifically for them.

- Rehearsing your elevator pitch, so you know exactly what message you want to give out at the event. Your elevator pitch includes a summary of your value proposition and summary of the client personas you are looking for. You want to make it easy for potential referral partners to refer work to you.

Good networking behaviours

When at the event, there are some basic rules of good behaviour. Show genuine interest in others by listening actively and asking thoughtful questions. Building rapport is key to gaining referrals and the best way to build rapport is to listen. Most people like talking about themselves so ask about what they do. The information you obtain will tell you if they are a good potential referral partner and also whether you like them enough to want to work together.

Repeat your elevator pitch to everyone you meet, even to the extent that you are bored of saying it by the end of the event. If you are standing in a group of people, do not be embarrassed about repeating it to new people who join the group. Explain what it is you do and what clients you are looking for. Less is more: have a memorable line to deliver when you meet someone: 'I am the lawyer who makes medtech start-up fundraising enjoyable'.

What is the point of these interactions? In the long run, it is to make great referral partners. But you have an immediate objective, which is to obtain the person's contact details. Add them to the networking funnel to follow up with them subsequently.

You do not have to become best buddies with them at the event. A 2018 study by Jeffrey A. Hall, a professor at the University of Kansas, looked at the time it takes to become friends. He identifies three stages of friendship. It takes 50 hours of quality contact as mere acquaintances to reach even the first stage, what he calls casual friendship. At the lower end of the networking funnel, all of your interactions will be with acquaintances. If you do it right, one or two of your referral partners may eventually become what Hall calls good friends (90 hours) or close friends (200 hours). Making close friends is not a specific objective of your referral strategy. Accept that you are dealing with acquaintances so do not spend all of an event talking to one person and do not be offended if they do not immediately accept your invitation to tea.

To ensure you keep moving and aren't trapped in conversations which are neither useful nor interesting, use this line: 'I'd really like to know more about that so could we exchange contact details and I'll follow up with you about it?' It makes it clear that you are moving on, obtains contact details and does not force you to make frequent trips to the bar or washroom.

Exchange business cards, email, LinkedIn or other social media details, depending on your sector. We prefer LinkedIn, as it is built for business networking.

The long game

For those less confident with approaching strangers at networking events, consider the long game. Talking to few people at an event is not inefficient if it improves your ability to network at subsequent events. Your sector will only have so many people in it, of which only a fraction will attend networking events. Over time, you will see the same people at these events. If you have only two in-depth conversations, they will stand you in good stead for the next event. You will not be walking into a room full of strangers. You will naturally join their conversation and meet who they are talking to.

The long game is slow but you meet people who like the people you like, which makes it sustainable: you will want to go to the next event to see them. It is accretive too, as the more you do it, the more people you will know. Assuming you are at the right networking event, most attendees will be useful in some way. So go to networking events to have fun with people you like. The best connections – and work – will flow from that. Be kind to yourself and don't compare yourself to those who can make friends and referral partners more quickly.

Reciprocity debt

Once you have found someone who meets your criteria of a good potential referral partner, start the relationship well by setting the pattern of behaviour. We humans are geared, almost automatically, to feel the need to reciprocate. If you want referrals, build up reciprocity debt in your new contacts so that they feel a low-level sense of obligation towards you. Do this by making introductions. You are unlikely to have a client for them right away, but you will know someone to introduce to them who will add value for their business. If you can introduce them to someone else at the event itself, so much the better: you'll be remembered as the person they want to be around at the next event. The more introductions you give out, the more reciprocity debt you build up. Everyone will know what to expect from the relationship.

The end of the networking funnel: follow-up

The networking funnel continues after the event is long finished. As Legal Geek founder, Jimmy Vestbirk says, failing to follow up promptly after an event is the commonest networking mistake. You have done the hard work of actually going to the event, meeting great referral partners and then not capitalised on it. The process is labour intensive if you do it manually, so automate this as much as possible.

We discuss systematising your networking efforts in the next chapter. Your networking funnel, like your referral strategy more generally, is dependent on efficient workflows and implementing the right technology solutions.

Systematise your referral programmes to grow your business

Mike Adams, introstars

Mike Adams, founder of introstars, wants to change the way we think about referrals. 'Most people spend 95 percent on cold outreach and 5 percent on referrals,' he says, 'which should be the other way around.'

introstars empowers B2B salespeople, agency owners, start-up founders, property developers and entrepreneurs (which he calls introseekers to emphasise that they are more than just a passive recipient) to generate leads. They do this through paid referral programmes with a wide reach where everyone can make a warm referral as an introducer. Referral programmes have always existed, he explains, and referral commissions are usually standard, except in the legal and public sector.

Even though referral programmes are common, most businesses focus these on their existing clients, and do not advertise them openly to reach a wider network of potential referral partners and introducers. There is also some reticence about referral commissions. Mike thinks this is more pronounced in Europe, where paid introductions are perceived as corrupting business relationships, than in the United States, where things are more transactional and it is commonly accepted to be compensated for a successful introduction. Most paid referral programmes are typically based on gentlemen's agreements, informal emails, or overly complicated terms and conditions. Either way most referrals are not properly tracked and there's no guarantee the introducer will get paid a referral commission.

introstars makes it easy to set up a referral programme in just a few clicks, where an introseeker describes their ideal customer profile and sets their reward for successful introductions. Once the introseeker has created and posted their referral programme, others on the platform can introduce them to potential clients. The aim of the introstars platform is to broadcast the referral programme far and wide to attract a huge array of introducers to send you more referrals. introstars makes it easy to track and pay out for inbound referrals. The aim, Mike says, is not just to rely on your existing contacts, but to actively expand your network of introducers.

Introseekers can set their own rewards, with an average of 10 percent of the deal size. It depends on the profit margin of the business paying the fee, which will be different depending on the sector, as well as the overall monetary value of the deal. If a profit margin is thin, the introseeker will usually pay a smaller percentage of the deal as a reward. For other industries where services are sold at nearly pure profit, the fee can be as high as 30 to 40 percent. For super large deals, the percentage might be 2-3 percent, which still represents a large reward for the introducer.

Mike sees a referral reward as a way of fairly compensating introducers who are creating genuine value for the introseeker and for the client. The initial incentive for the introducer to make a referral must be to truly help the client and the introseeker. 'If you make crappy introductions, the intro won't work, you won't get paid anyway and your reputation will deteriorate.' The referral reward is a fair compensation for the introducer: Mike says that if you are putting your reputation on the line and providing genuine economic value, you deserve to be paid. Otherwise there is a lot of value in the transaction, and the economy as a whole, that is not being paid for. It is an interesting thought: how different would GDP figures be if they allocated a monetary value to referrals?

Mike wants to change the way people think about lead generation. He wants businesses to rethink their lead-gen strategy to move away from 'spammy cold outreach', and instead refocus their efforts around warm introductions and referral programmes. Mike expects cold outreach to die out as AI becomes increasingly adept at filtering out spam. Warm referrals are the future of lead generation, he believes.

10

SCALE REFERRALS
WITH TECHNOLOGY

Service businesses need technology to systematically grow their business through referrals. Anyone can make informal, ad hoc referrals but that is not the path to sustainable growth. It takes time to make introductions, respond to emails and organise catch ups. It is hard to remember who has referred what to whom. It is hard to remember simple things like your referral partners' birthdays or the names of their children.

Referrals are hard to scale because trust is hard to scale. If you try to do it manually, after a while, you will stop focusing on referrals as a strategy. Referrals will become a nice to have rather than an engine of growth. That is a waste. Technology does not just make your life easier: it allows you to know your clients and referral partners better, spot patterns and grow. As tech start-ups like introstars show, there is technology available specifically designed to facilitate referrals.

To use technology to scale your referral strategy, we will look at:

- Workflows

- Customer or client relationship management (CRM) tools

- Automations

- Templates

- Scheduling and communication tools

- Data analytics and reporting

What follows is not a survey of the latest technology available. That would not age well. Instead, at the end of this chapter, you will understand the importance of workflows and referral technology to grow your business.

Artificial intelligence is all pervasive and increasingly capable of performing many of the tasks described in this chapter. You still need to understand what the underlying processes are so that you know what to ask your powerful AI assistant to do. Imagine hiring a talented junior marketing executive and having no idea what you want them to achieve. Your leadership is still required.

As start-ups like introstars and developments in AI show, technology does not stand still. Hopefully, neither will your business, which means that you do not have time to keep on top of the constant change. Falling behind is not an option for a successful business. To exploit tech to its full potential and avoid becoming stale, hire outside help and train yourself and your team. Reassuringly, perhaps, we humans still have our uses. It takes time to design your workflows, implement your automations and review your data. So even though we're talking about tech, we're talking about people too. This chapter is not about tech replacing people, but about tech enabling people and people enabling tech.

Workflows and data

Before you invest in tech, review how you currently work, what data you collect and how it is stored. The best tech in the world will not correct for bad processes and incomplete data. The bigger your organisation, the harder it becomes. The review will highlight whether your processes just need to be improved or need a complete overhaul.

Use a workflow mapping tool like Miro to draw out a flow chart of what you want to happen, including all the contingencies, down to the granular detail. If a person doesn't respond to your email, what is the next stage in the process? You will use this to set up the CRM and design your automations.

To implement it, you may need marketing and development experts who understand CRMs and your referral strategy. They will save you time, allowing you to focus on billable client work. Talk with them about your workflow, amend it, then work with them to put it in place.

Your referral strategy is personal and built around you, so project manage this workflow process yourself. Think of technology as your exoskeleton: it will give you a superpower, but it needs to fit.

Customer relationship management

The starting point is your CRM. It allows you to store your data in one place, identify your best referrers and communicate easily with them. CRMs usually include the following features:

- Workflows and automations

- Email and social media templates

- Newsletters

- Sync with email and collaboration tools

- Reports and analytics

- Data security

CRMs vary widely in price. To begin with we would recommend using an inexpensive option that includes these features, and upgrade as and when required. You will find that you do not need to use all of the features available. Setting up your CRM is the hardest stage, so we would recommend investing in some help here. You cannot delegate it away entirely, however. It is your responsibility to understand what the CRM can do and to understand the new workflows. Use the opportunity to train yourself and other members of your team how to use the CRM properly.

For a referral strategy you will need slightly different data to a normal sales strategy. You will collect data about both clients and referrers in order to help identify the client and referrer personas we discussed earlier. The basic data you want is:

- **Full name**

- **Business name**

- **Name for correspondence**: many people do not use their first name as their given name.

- **Sector**: such as hospitality or oil and gas.

- **Profession**: this is detail about the person, rather than their business. If a person is the chief marketing officer at a food delivery company, their profession is marketing.

- **Specialism**: if a person's profession is marketing, their specialism might be SEO or website design.

- **Where we met:** recording this will show you what your best events are for finding good referral partners.

- **When we met**: this is important so you can calculate metrics like client lifetime value.

- **Introduced by**: if you know the links between your network it is easier to arrange events and invite people who know each other.

- **Introduced to**: update this data field with every introduction from the referrer to you.

- **Client value**: this is the value of fees paid directly by this person or their organisation to you.

- **Client persona**: this should be the client persona you have identified that best fits with this client.

- **Referrer persona**: record the RP separately from the client persona as same person may be both and your categories will be different for clients and referrers.

- **Number of referrals**: the number of paying clients referred by this person to your business. Aggregating this number with others of the same referrer persona will allow you to calculate the RP referrals number and the average RP referrals.

- **Referrer billings**: the fees paid by clients referred to your business by this person. Aggregating this number with others of the same RP will allow you to calculate the RP billings and the average RP billings.

This data will allow you to identify your best client and referrer personas, calculated against the metrics we have discussed. It allows you to analyse where your best work comes from and which events to attend. By collecting the client value for each person in your CRM and combining it with your introduced-to data, you will see the value of each RP to your business for any given period. You then calculate the billings for each RP.

As important, your automations and templates will be personalised by this data. Messages like thank you emails can be triggered when you update the introduced-to data field, so you always thank people in a timely fashion.

Automations

If you thought that the advice about leveraging marketing and contacting key partners was time consuming, this is where we relieve that anxiety. Create automations that periodically contact clients and referral partners with newsletters and bespoke emails, based on templates which draw in their data from your system.

The automations you enact will depend on the workflows you have devised for your business. To show you what these might look like, let's consider two labour-intensive workflows that benefit from automation:

- following up with clients after a piece of work has been completed;

- following up with contacts after a networking event.

Client follow-up

A simple automated workflow should look like this:

- After the project has concluded, show that you go the extra mile to improve your service by asking for feedback on the work you have done. It will help you improve what you do and sets up the conversation where you ask your clients for further referral opportunities. Ask if they are happy to be added to your mailing list.

- Two months later, ask for a catch-up to discuss how their business is going. Remind them of the work you do and ask for further referral opportunities.

- Six months later, email them asking to arrange a coffee. Repeat this every six months.

This is all automated, so there is no extra work for you other than the conversation with the client. Clients love it and you can find out about their business and whether they need help with anything else.

Networking follow-up

Imagine you meet ten people at an event and you want to follow up with them. That means ten emails saying how great it was to meet them and how you'd like to arrange a call. Then there are up to ten replies with times and dates, and so on. Each is bespoke, depending on how the person responds. It is so maddeningly laborious that you probably do not do it and your networking strategy is undermined.

The first hack is to use the LinkedIn app QR code at events to exchange details. Ensure you are the person showing your QR code and allow the other person to scan it, so that they send you the connection request. You will see on your app whether the request has worked and can accept it immediately. It reduces the opportunity for error on their part. When you accept the request send them this message and let them see you write it: 'great to meet you at [the event] and talk about [subject]'. It reminds both of you the next day and makes it clear that you have been listening to them.

As soon as possible afterwards, input the person into your CRM, or have your assistant or AI do this for you. Interfaces (APIs) are available for connecting to your LinkedIn. Have an automation set up on your CRM as follows:

- As soon as you or a member of your team inputs the contact's data from a networking event, an email is sent to them automatically, addressed to them personally, referring to the event where you met, with a link to book a 15-minute call in your calendar. Bear in mind that spam filters may catch emails containing hyperlinks.

- If they do not respond within a few days, a gentle reminder email is sent out automatically.

- Hopefully, the person then books a call. If they do not, that's on them. As you have not invested too much time in this process, you do not need to worry too much if they do not respond.

Number of bespoke emails? None.

Template and AI-generated communications

Automations would mean nothing if you had to write a new message each time. Writing emails is laborious, even when the content is not new. Each message requires consideration of your tone, how the recipient might react and how best to elicit the response you want. Writers' block is a problem for the writers of emails as much as for the authors of novels. For introverts, it is a draining exercise, as it carries with it a measure of social risk. Simple emails drop to the bottom of the to-do list, which hurts your business if you rely on referrals for work. It makes you look inefficient or that you don't value the person who has contacted you.

To avoid this cycle of social anxiety, delay and disappointment, use templates. Many bespoke emails are different combinations of standard responses, so prepare them in advance. The best way to prepare a template email is to write it to one person in a real situation and save that email. To get you started, ask AI to write the first draft.

Save these templates in your email provider for easy access. For example, Microsoft Outlook has a handy templates' feature that enables you to respond quickly to emails. You'll avoid that social anxiety and writers' block.

To make the best of your templates, combine them with the data and automations in your CRM so that your emails will populate with the relevant names and other data. You will never need to send a chaser email again. Your emails will be personalised, timely and will not require any further input from you. You do, however, need to turn the chaser emails off when the person responds and most CRMs automate this too.

Here are some of the basic email templates for your referral strategy:

- introducing one contact to another;

- thanking a referrer for an introduction to a service provider and setting up a call;

- thanking a referrer for an introduction to a client and setting up a call;

- asking contacts for recommendations for particular services;

- asking contacts if they can do the work that needs doing;

- asking clients or contacts for a catch-up call;

- following up after meeting a person at an event to set up a one-to-one;

- email to a contact who does not attend an online meeting or call;
- reminders in relation to any of the above emails.

To get you started, templates for these emails are included as an appendix. Even armed with these templates, there will be moments requiring genuinely bespoke responses. For these times, use AI. AI is particularly powerful if you already have templates set up, because you can ask it to respond to an email in your tone and style based on your existing templates.

Scheduling, communication and collaboration tools

It is difficult to keep on top of all of the tools available to the modern business. There are several categories of app which are great weapons in the armoury of the referral strategy.

Scheduling apps

Your referral strategy is all about building know, like and trust, which involves considerable face time. Use scheduling apps to reduce the time it takes to organise these meetings. These include standalone apps like Calendly or those which integrate with your email or CRM providers. They avoid the back and forth of booking a call and make them easier to arrange. They are a great example of using technology to bring people together. Use them like this:

- set up your calendar in the app to show when you are available;
- the calendar will sync with the other calendars you use, so if you have other meetings come in, no one will be able to double book;

- when you want to arrange a call with someone else, send someone a link to your diary;

- they click on the link to see what times are available and book in a call;

- if you or they need to rearrange, it is easy to do so.

When sending the link, write: 'if convenient please use this link to find a time that works for you. Alternatively, let me know when suits'. Some people are resistant to any kind of change, so don't force them to do something they don't want to. Give them the option to arrange the meeting the old-fashioned way. Most will click the link.

Think carefully about your app settings. Do not allow calls to be booked throughout the day, otherwise you will find yourself constantly interrupted by calls. If you like planning out your day in the morning, change your settings so that people cannot book a call with you on the same day that they make the appointment. Otherwise, you'll miss meetings booked after you set out your daily schedule. Keep the calls short to discourage blather and ensure there is always a gap between calls. It avoids being late for subsequent calls and gives you a breather.

Video conferencing

Use platforms like Zoom or Microsoft Teams for virtual meetings with referral partners, making it easier to connect regardless of location. Ubiquitous during the pandemic, these platforms are still gamechangers. They are not as good as in-person interactions, but they are better than purely written or oral communications.

Integrate your video conferencing with an AI notetaker and you'll find yourself awash with information to be dropped into your CRM.

Before each call, use AI to provide a summary of your previous conversations, including any action points agreed on or important dates and names. You'll be the best-informed person on the call.

To make them more sustainable, turn the video off. MIT research has established that it reduces your environmental footprint by 96 percent.

Messaging apps

Use apps like WhatsApp, Slack or Teams for quick and efficient communication with your team and referral partners. CRMs and other tools integrate with popular messaging apps in the same way as they do with email.

Data analytics and reporting

Data paints a picture. The higher quality data you collect, the better picture you will have of the effectiveness of your referral strategy, which is important to:

- Track performance: use analytics tools within your CRM to track the performance of your referral strategy using your key metrics.

- Track referrals: use your CRM to understand which events and contacts provide value.

- Generate reports: create regular reports to analyse performance and identify your key referrer personas.

- Adjust strategies: use insights from your analytics to refine and improve your referral process over time.

To make sure you have the right data, set up your CRM to collect information in relation to referrals, as well as individual contacts and businesses. Record inbound and outbound referrals to give you a complete picture of your referral activity.

A referral deal should include the following data fields:

- Who made the referral.

- To whom the referral was made.

- When the referral was made.

- What work the referral related to.

- Date of first invoice.

- Fees generated. If you are the recipient of the referral, you will know this exactly. For outbound referrals, include an estimate.

- Reason for failure. If the referral falls through, record why.

Collecting information on a deal-by-deal basis is useful, but becomes incredibly powerful when collated with all your other deal information. From this pool of data you will be able to see, among other things:

- The total value of fees from referrals.

- Seasonality (if any).

- The success rate of referrals.

- The average length of time from introduction to invoice.

The average RP referrals and average RP billings are the key information in relation to referrals but seeing the raw data per referrer and per referral is useful too. It enables you to deploy the other strategies we have talked about in this book. You will take your best referrers out to dinner or celebrate them on LinkedIn. You'll be able to take the client and referrer out for dinner at any celebratory moments during the course of the work. It also provides clues if your referral strategy is not working as planned.

On the subject of data, it's worth emphasising the importance of cybersecurity and data protection. Wherever you are in the world, you have legal obligations to look after your contacts' data. If you work across borders, you are likely to be subject to several different data protection regimes. Either way you should have proper data protection protocols and cyber security in place. You must be cautious using AI and understand what happens to your clients' data when you do. While you want to avoid fines, the main reason for good behaviour is because it is good for your clients and therefore good for you. Compliance is confidence building among clients and referral partners. A data protection or cybersecurity breach will seriously undermine even the best referral strategy.

Augmented collaboration

Technology is key to building a referral strategy that grows your business over the long term, so long as it amplifies real human interaction and does not seek to replace it. A referral strategy that feels impersonal will not help grow your business. The value of a referral is that it is a recommendation from one human being to another, based on knowing, liking and trusting each other. The goal is to find repetitive tasks and replace them with automations and templates, while using data to find your best referral partners faster. You will meet more of the right people, obtain valuable referrals and enjoy it. You'll need to keep learning though: technology does not stand still and neither should you.

The dark side of referrals

Kasvi Seghal, Law.com International

Kasvi Sehgal, journalist at Law.com International, has helped expose the darker side of referrals among big law firms. It relates to the practice of designation in private equity deals, which involves the private equity client and their lawyer (on one side of a transaction) picking the lawyer for the bank on the other side of a transaction. It's as dodgy as it sounds, like the manager of a football team picking the goalkeeper for the other side.

Designation is an egregious type of referral, but it's still a referral: one professional referring work to another professional. Kasvi explains in more detail how it works. On a private equity deal, it is common for private equity firms to have strong relationships with certain law firms. Often the PE firm and their lawyers designate the legal team they want the bank to instruct, which gives them a lot of power.

The lawyers are all pals with each other. There are only a handful of firms that dominate this market in the United Kingdom and, within these firms, there is only a small group of lawyers who closely work with private equity firms and use designation. They are nearly all men. You can tell who the best friends are: Kasvi says she frequently sees the same circles on the sponsor and lender sides using this model, so it is possible to gauge which PE firm or adviser is biased against whom.

The banks put up with it because they trust the legal profession to act in their clients' best interests. But Kasvi says that there is a concern within the industry that the lender side's counsel appease the private equity lawyers to maintain their relationship. One of the ways they might do this is by deliberately avoiding negotiating too hard. It's an obvious conflict of interest, or as, Kasvi puts it 'a rigged game of monopoly'.

Kasvi says that appropriate authorities need to look at this practice more carefully to ensure that business is being conducted in an ethical way. Until then, the practice continues and will do so as long as a small group of influential individuals controls access to a specialised area of legal advice.

11

BEST-LAID PLANS

'Everyone has a plan,' according to boxer and occasional sage, Mike Tyson, 'until they get punched in the mouth'. When it comes to a referral strategy, the pain is often self-inflicted.

We're now going to look at some of the common bad behaviours that cause referrals to fail and trust to break down. We have set out how to build a referral strategy. But for it to succeed, we need to stop punching ourselves in the mouth. Broadly we can split our bad referral behaviours into three categories:

- Bad quality

- Bad value

- Bad communication

A bad referral partner may well display all three of these behaviours and if the quality of your work is bad, you are, by definition, providing bad value. But it is the third category where service providers inexcusably fall down, even those professionals whose entire careers are based on communication. All of us will have displayed some of these behaviours during our careers.

It's worth noting how strange this is. So many professional businesses rely on referrals, inbound and outbound, to grow. But then we act in a way almost guaranteed to stop us receiving additional referrals. It is that observation that first sparked the idea for this book. We are not trained how to collaborate, so we make basic errors.

That would just be an inconvenience, except that bad referrals hurt your bottom line and reputation. We all like to think we have a good reputation, because the people who like us do refer work to us. The truth is there will be many people who don't think that we are great and do not refer us additional work. Most of the time we will never know anything about it, so our professional ego is essentially built on survivor bias. Those missed opportunities are potentially worth hundreds of thousands of pounds. They are the difference between survival or not, between thriving and just limping along.

If you have a bad experience with a referral, you will be more reticent next time. Maybe you'll try to do the work yourself, maybe you won't reach out for help until it's too late. Bad referrals poison the well for the whole village and deter people from collaborating in future. That is bad for professionals and bad for clients. So let's look at these self-harming behaviours that throw a right hook to the face of your referral strategy.

Bad quality

We all pride ourselves on being good at our jobs, but we have all fallen short on occasion. Bad quality work varies from bad-quality presentation to negligence. Let's start with that worst-case scenario.

Negligence

Negligence is the professional's greatest fear. Merely an accusation of negligence can be career ending, not least because the stress can cause people to leave their profession. It is also expensive, because even if you are insured, your premiums will increase. Sometimes you might have to work for free to fix the mistake. The fear of an accusation of negligence can make professionals maddeningly risk averse.

All negligence comes down to a mistake, and every service provider and every client knows that everyone makes mistakes. The pretence at perfection is dangerous and self-defeating. Clients are surprisingly generous when errors are made, provided you are honest about them and have a plan to fix them. Indeed, coming to a client with a plan to fix your mistake can even raise you in their estimation.

So if you make a mistake for the client, don't stick your head in the sand. Own up to it, notify your insurers, come up with a plan and tell the client. Do it all as soon as possible. Sometimes it won't be enough, and maybe the client will bad mouth you to their contacts or worse, but at least you'll have done your best and you'll be able to sleep at night. Your reputation might take a knock, but at least your honesty cannot be questioned.

Dishonesty

People lie. Some professions are more suspect than others. Politicians, journalists, estate agents and even lawyers are often seen as untrustworthy. Every person on the planet has lied at some point in their life. But in business, if you are not trusted, people won't work with you. So if you do lie to your clients: stop. If you don't want to stop, then let me know so I can avoid working with you in future.

There is a grey area though, where you don't lie but you're not transparent either. Maybe you do make a mistake and manage to fix it without needing to tell the client. Why do they need to know? Perhaps you missed an email and caused a delay, why admit it? Perhaps, like the lawyers in Kasvi's example above, you have a conflict of interest and don't negotiate as hard as you should for your clients. Then again, maybe you are just having the morning off to look after your children, but you tell a client you are unavailable because you are in a meeting.

If you want to show your clients, and the person who referred them to you, that you are trustworthy, be transparent about the small and big things alike. Clients and referrers will know you have a life outside work and that you will make mistakes. You are only human. What will set you apart is your honesty. If you can't be honest with your client about having to look after your own children, you are working for the wrong client, and you don't want referrers to send you clients like that.

Presentation

If your presentation is poor, clients and referrers will assume the quality is poor too. You wouldn't go to a client meeting dressed only in your underwear, so don't bare all your metaphorical lumps and bumps either. The biggest presentational mistakes to correct now are:

- **Your profile photograph**: whether on LinkedIn or your website, for potential referral partners who haven't met you yet, you are your photograph. It is what they think of when they think of you. If it's fuzzy, unclear, facing to the side or looking overly casual, you're giving a terrible impression to your referral partners.

- **Your website**: it's your shop window. Even if you don't receive much work through it, it is nonetheless where referral partners will go to check you out. A bad website makes a terrible impression.

- **Your writing**: your style matters. If your spelling and grammar are bad, make sure you're using the grammar and spell checks in your correspondence. Social media, like WhatsApp, are more like a written conversation, but emails occupy a strange territory between formal letter and phone call. The first priority is to spell someone's name right.

- **Formatting**: there is a profession dedicated to designing fonts, called type designers. Show them some respect and use their fonts consistently. While we're at it, sort your font size, paragraphs and (for lawyers) clause numbering too.

Lack of commerciality and poor understanding of risk

People come to you to fix their problem. Some service providers, and we lawyers can be the worst at this, are risk averse and often lack commerciality. Lawyers sometimes advise our clients to avoid all risk, ignoring commercial reality. Legal risk is often not the biggest concern for a business. For a start-up, for example, the biggest risk is not that someone will steal their intellectual property, it is that their genius idea is, in fact, rubbish.

When referring a client to another service provider, it is frustrating when the recipient overengineers their solution, out of proportion to the risk or opportunity involved. These referral partners lack a sense of what the client actually wants, and act as if their area of expertise is the only one that matters. They fail to realise that while they are an expert, they are not the expert in the client's business or their life. Their advice completely misunderstands the client's priorities.

Just as annoying is the indecisive adviser. If we don't advise the client on a way out of their problem and just say 'on the one hand, on the other hand', we service providers have failed in our jobs. The client will feel like they have not moved any further forward. Frustration with this approach was one of the main reasons for setting up Adviserly. Lawyers at boutique law firms tend to be more entrepreneurial and decisive than those at big firms, because we run our own businesses.

That being said, on the other hand, gung-ho advisers are worse. No one wants to refer their clients to another professional who dabbles in areas where they do more harm than good; it is a common cause of negligence and also causes stress for the dabbler.

Stick to your area of competence and expand your expertise only gradually. You'll remain confident and commercial, as well as avoid being too risk averse or too gung-ho. The better your referral strategy, the more you receive clients that fit your skillset. The better your risk analysis, the happier your clients will be.

Bad value

Service providers have different price points. There is no such thing as a usual market price, particularly across borders, currencies and cultures. Some charge fixed fees or by the hour. Tax lawyers charge more than builders, but a builder in Manhattan might charge the same as a tax lawyer in Sudan. So it is not straightforward. But when you see a quote for work that you know the client will hate, it is frustrating.

The quote does not match the work or the client

Pricing professional work is a skill. Should we price by time, by value delivered or by the ability of the client to pay? While many books have been written on this subject, ultimately, the market price is however much you can get away with. And that therefore needs to take in value delivered and ability to pay. Unless the system is rigged in some way, as with designations in the private equity legal market, you earn high fees only if you provide great value. Equally, if the client can't pay, high fees are unpaid fees. The more experience you have at quoting, the better you will be at pricing your work.

There is a difference between the value your business provides and the time you spend doing the work. For the client, your time is irrelevant. It is only relevant for you in determining whether it is cost effective for you to take on the work. Pricing by the hour might still be standard for your industry, but clients are increasingly unwilling to put up with it because it doesn't translate to value provided.

When you receive a referral, consider your costs in providing the work, the value to the client and their ability to pay. Then decide whether you have bandwidth to take on the work. If not, politely decline the referral. Don't cheapen your expertise and don't pretend to have skills that you lack. Offer a fee that matches the work and also matches the client. You'll show your referral partners you understand their clients and you'll highlight your own value in the process.

The referrer doesn't set fee expectations

Without an honest conversation about fees between referrer and recipient provider, there can be real dissonance between expectations and quote, leading to unhappiness all round. When asking for a quote, the referrer should set the fee range that they and their client expect. Do this informally: 'I think the client will be ok with £3000 to £4000, is that doable?' It prompts a conversation which means the provider can then tailor the service and explain whether such fee expectations are wrong. And what's more, it is amazing how often setting a range will result in the price you want.

Quoting without sufficient information

If you receive a referral request, it is a real struggle to provide a decent quote if the referrer or client doesn't give you the relevant information. If you don't provide the right background, expect an inaccurate quote. Treat your referral partners as you would like to be treated yourself. Give them enough information to provide accurate fee quotes. If you are receiving a referral on scant information, ask follow-up questions until you are in a position to provide an accurate quote.

Quote harvesting

Sometimes clients and their advisers are just harvesting quotes from other service providers to gauge the right price for a piece of work. It is at once completely reasonable but feels disrespectful if done brazenly. It often leads to insufficient information being provided and ghosting once the quote has been provided.

If you are quote harvesting, tell the service provider that you are seeking a range of quotes. It shows respect and allows them to decline to quote. If you or your client chooses to go elsewhere, let the unsuccessful bidder know, ideally with some constructive feedback.

Do not take offence if you are on the receiving end of someone who is quote harvesting. Ask for further information as needed and provide a quote as you normally would. If nothing else, you are building your referral relationship for the future. If you don't like wasting time in this situation, it may be that your quoting process is inefficient, which is your responsibility, not theirs. If you don't win the client, ask for feedback and then act on it.

Blowing the estimates

Once a client has instructed you, don't blow the estimate. If the scope of work changes, update the quote and keep the referrer informed, though make sure not to breach confidentiality. Poor communication on fees is the number one cause of disputes between advisers and clients. If you receive a referral and then anger the client by blowing the estimate, don't expect subsequent referrals.

Loss leaders

It is tempting not to charge full fees for referred work, particularly for large clients who hold out the prospect of high future fees. This makes sense if you are just starting out and need to pump prime your client base. Loss leaders also work for high-growth clients like start-ups who cannot pay full price now but will do in the future. For other clients, it is counterproductive. By failing to value your expertise properly, you encourage the client to do so too. The whole relationship is then based on discounted fees, rather than the value you provide.

Loss leaders are common for referrals in large organisations, where departments take on referrals from other teams for reasons of internal politics as much as for their bottom line. Loss leaders create stress for the team members, as the work will be less profitable and affect their billing targets and potential for bonuses. If you charge full price for subsequent projects, they can also cause a shock for the client. For most work therefore, avoid loss leaders.

Bad communication

Being ungrateful

This is the cardinal sin of the referral process. A referral from another service provider is a big thing. If they have sent work your way, say thank you. It is not hard, but if you don't do it, they'll remember. If you want to go the extra mile, send a small, non-financial gift.

As Daniel Coyle points out in *The Culture Code,* a thank you has a much wider impact than just the person to whom it is addressed: '… thank-yous aren't only expressions of gratitude; they're crucial belonging cues that generate a contagious sense of safety, connection and motivation'. Coyle cites research showing that receiving a thank you makes you behave 'far more generously' to others. The opposite is also true, so if you are ungrateful, expect to exist in a world of ingratitude.

No or slow responses

We have all been guilty of this but taking days to respond to a referral, or not responding at all, suggests either that you don't have time or that you think you are above the kind of work the referrer is trying to give you. They won't want to refer work to you again. At Adviserly, we have identified the following common reasons for delay:

- You're too busy now but you want the work later.

- The client isn't the right fit and you don't want the work, but you don't like disappointing people.

- You haven't been given enough information, but you don't have time to engage immediately and ask the right questions.

- You do not think there is a high chance of winning the work so you do not rush to organise the scoping call.

The key to all of these is to have a template email ready to go for the receipt of referrals, which takes away much of the thinking required before you reply. Replying sooner rather than later, even with a message turning down the work, shows you to be an efficient and decisive service provider who knows how to manage your time. Leave it too late and, however good your work is, you'll look disorganised or disrespectful.

Accepting work when you are too busy

If you are busy and take on work anyway, this can lead to terrible communication. It is hard to judge when good busy becomes bad busy, as client work has a habit of coming in waves. But much bad behaviour, including non-responses and bad quoting, is down to the recipient being too busy and then providing sub-par communication. Overpromising and underdelivering is poison to a healthy working relationship. Be prepared to say no, politely and quickly. Everyone will move on and be grateful you were honest.

Leaving it to the last minute to find good referral partners

Having built Adviserly from nothing to a thriving global network over three years, we know it takes a long time to find quality referral partners. Before setting up the network, I was reactive, looking for referral partners as and when needed by clients, which led to rushed communications, delays and stress.

So set up your network in advance and you will find that you are not, despite the title of this book, working with strangers. Communication becomes easier and the referral process speeds up. It becomes a pleasure to collaborate. You will be working with friends and colleagues.

Overcomplicating your referral process with non-solicitation agreements

Client poaching is a real issue, but the best defence against it is offering great value. When I first became a partner at a law firm, I worried about this and wanted to make sure my referral partners signed up to non-compete or non-solicitation agreements, which was overkill. Instead, focus on building a group of referral partners who you trust not to poach your clients.

Repairing trust

It might seem odd for a book called *Working with Strangers* to argue that the best way to stop self-sabotaging your referral strategy is to stop working with strangers. Get to know, like and trust your referral partners and the issues of quality, value and communication identified in this chapter will be easier to resolve. You will be able to have honest conversations with your partners and help each other improve. This feels old fashioned in the age of artificial intelligence, but human weaknesses cannot be magicked away with a well phrased AI prompt. It takes real effort and courage to fix damaged relationships.

The tragedy is that when we come across bad behaviours in others, it deters us from trusting and collaborating at all. Adopting the mantra of once bitten, twice shy, we are leaving opportunities on the table. We can't expect our referral strategy to work if we are punching ourselves in the mouth, but nor will we succeed if we leave the ring altogether. Labelling our own bad behaviour is the first step to stopping it. Admitting our faults to each other is the first step to repairing the trust that such behaviour destroys and being able to move forward to collaborate with confidence.

CONCLUSION:
THE AUDACITY OF TRUST

In *Working with Strangers*, we have shown how to deploy the humble referral to further your career and grow your business. A referral is a powerful thing: someone trusts you enough to risk their reputation and introduce a potential client to you. Referrals provide you with the best clients: those who already understand what you do and trust you. By building a referral strategy you are systematising what you are already doing ad hoc. It is therefore the easiest way to grow your business and you can start today.

A referral is a business transaction, but it is also a personal interaction that depends on knowing, liking and trusting the other person. Collaborating in this way reinforces those relationships which are the foundation of a thriving career or business. You get to know each other, share information and learn. Referrals help build a sense of reciprocity, community and comradeship. This is especially true for complex referrals. Collaboration helps us move from transactional cognitive trust to heart-led affective trust with partners who may become friends. Collaboration is the key to healthy functioning of all communities.

Communities, including small businesses and charities, are vital to a healthy economy and environment. The 18th-century Irish philosopher, Edmund Burke (often called the father of conservatism, but don't let that put you off), observed that:

> To be attached to the subdivision, to love the little platoon
> we belong to in society, is the first principle (the germ as
> it were) of public affections. It is the first link in the series
> by which we proceed towards a love to our country and
> to mankind.

In other words, we collaborate in small groups first and those groups collaborate with each other. In smaller groups we have more control, more agency and are more in touch with our humanity. In service businesses, these smaller groups are your team, your clients and your referral partners.

Whatever their form, these communities spread economic power out from the centre, away from the super-rich and political insiders towards the little platoons. Rather than being a cog in a machine, to whom things happen, people are empowered when they work in small communities. Small businesses make decisions locally, in keeping with their locality and environment.

That doesn't mean communities have to stay small. In his book, *Value(s)*, former Bank of England governor, Mark Carney, talks of 'artisanal globalisation'. He argues that small businesses, armed with technology like 3D printers and the referral tools we have talked about in this book, will cease to need the infrastructure of big business to supply goods and services around the world. Empowered by our referral partners, we will become increasingly adept at working with strangers and growing our careers and businesses in ways that work for us. We are on our way to a world where clusters of empowered communities collaborate across borders. That is what Adviserly was set up to do. This book was written to help get us there. Just because platoons are small doesn't make them insular: if we link arms we can reach around the world.

As many service business owners tell me, their priority is not necessarily growth. The aim is to thrive. Collaboration makes business sustainable by providing a network of encouragement and support in lean times. Growth is part of the picture, but in balance with your family and your way of life, team and community. Covid lockdowns have opened many peoples' eyes: there is more to life than becoming ever richer. It is timely, because we are reaching, or have already blundered over, the limits of non-stop growth. There is only so much the planet can take. In *Doughnut Economics,* Kate Raworth urges us to recognise these limits and, in place of growth, prioritise thriving within the limits of our ambition, our energy and our other priorities.

The challenges we face are very real, so we do have to link arms. There are big forces at play: climate change, species loss, the looming threat of war, famine and mass migration. These are issues that can only be tackled by the little platoons acting together. Remember the healed shin bone that Margaret Mead reportedly gave as early evidence of civilisation. We need that simple but powerful spirit of collaboration now more than ever.

Many of us place our hope in technology or government to combat these challenges. The future seems to be one dominated by artificial intelligence which will revolutionise, for good or ill, how people work

and live. Perhaps technology will break us free of the Malthusian trap that we have escaped so many times before. It has always been a bad idea to bet against human ingenuity, but confidence makes us complacent too. As our challenges grow, we rely more on computers and place increasing powers into the hands of governments and international bodies. AI and supposedly trustless systems like blockchain do not require personal connection or community. As individuals, it feels like none of it is our problem to solve and we could do nothing about it even if it were.

If the future is just computers and governments talking to each other, what is the point in people? To avoid this impersonal dystopia, we need to work together efficiently and strategically. A referral strategy is not just a way to build a thriving career or business. It is key to building a collaboration economy, in which we build a future based on people talking to and trusting people, enabled by technology rather than replaced by it, telling governments and big corporations what we need rather than the other way around.

We can do it if we trust each other, because trust is audacious. Trust is both inherently unreasonable but also a defining part of what it means to be human. It makes collaboration and change possible, but it springs spontaneously from collaboration too. It all starts by working with strangers, but it does not end there.

APPENDIX 1

SUMMARY:
THE REFERRAL STRATEGY

Principles

- While collaboration starts by working with strangers, the aim is to build referral relationships with partners you come to know like and trust so that you stop working with strangers as soon as possible.

- A recommendation from someone a client trusts is powerful because it responds to their sense of jeopardy and narrows their choice of service provider. Clients who come to you by way of a recommendation already trust you to help them achieve their goals, because they trust the person who referred them to you.

- Trust, but verify. Trust your referral partners generously, but only up to a certain point. We cannot assume our referral partners or our clients know what they are doing. Gather information on our partners and update our opinion as the facts change. Trust makes collaboration and change possible, but it springs spontaneously from collaboration too.

- Your referral partners enhance your business resilience. When your business goes through a tough patch, it is your friends and partners in business who will help pull you through.

- Collaboration is a skill that takes training and practice, and, if you want to grow your business by referrals, a strategy is required.

- By giving service providers the power to choose to work together on different projects, referrals, especially complex ones, are at the heart of a thriving collaboration economy, in which we build a future based on people talking to and trusting people, enabled by technology.

Qualifying referrals

- Fire-and-forget referral = recommendation + introduction

- When you receive a referral request, first establish whether a fire-and-forget referral or a complex referral is required. Does your client just want to be introduced to a third party or do they want you to project manage?

- Before making a referral, establish the client's objective: know what they want to achieve and that will shape who you introduce them to. Determine whether good price, good quality or fast delivery are the priorities for your client.

- Use the BTOP method of referral qualification to determine if the referral is a hot referral by identifying if a prospect's budget, team, other parties and planning are aligned before making a referral.

- The selection of the right service provider for a client is where referrers come into their own. Like a matchmaker, referrers are performing a nuanced and delicate task, taking into account their knowledge of both sides.

- If you are the recipient of the referral and the referrer has not followed the BTOP referral qualification steps, do this yourself. Check the client's deadlines, ensure you have the skills and capacity to act, speak to the referrer, follow up with clients after you have sent them a quote, onboard the client promptly and do not step on the toes of the referrer.

- Once you have made a referral, build your professional reputation and the quality of your referral network by asking the client how well the referral partner has responded to their needs.

Complex referrals

- Complex referral = recommendation + introduction + teamwork

- Ask the client or the lead service provider how much project management they want you to do. Make it clear how much work is involved in project management.

- If you become the project manager of a complex referral, the buck stops with you. Use a steps plan actively and dynamically to make your job easier. Don't rely solely on interactive collaboration tools.

- On a cross-border multicultural team, have as few people in the group work across cultures as possible. If your goal is innovation or creativity, the more cultural diversity the better; if your goal is simple speed and efficiency, then monocultural teams are probably better.

- If you find yourself on a team with poor-quality legacy advisers, inform the client so that they have the opportunity to change the team. As you do not know the strength of the relationship between the client and their existing service providers, be delicate in how you approach the subject.

- After the big completion moment, arrange a call with the client to congratulate them and reinforce the relationship, while also using the opportunity to remind them of the post-completion and admin work that still needs doing.

Identify your referral personality type

- A referral strategy is built around people, not algorithms or artificial intelligence. Spend some time to consider who you are, why you do what you do and what your negotiating style is. Everyone has the potential to be a great referrer, even shy introverts.

- Consider your motivations and those of your referral partners to better align your referral relationships. Are you a default career professional, mission-led or an obsessive?

- What is your negotiating style? Consider whether you are an assertive, an accommodator or an analyst so you can understand how you interact with partners and clients in a work setting, and who you like working with.

- Understand the role of your culture in determining the way you think and behave, how this affects your referral partners and clients too and the way you perceive and behave towards each other.

Your ideal client and value proposition

- Find a niche. It is easier to know your target client and value proposition if you are a specialist or operate in a particular sector.

- Establish your client personas by traits, such as behaviour, geographic location or demography to help you think about your current and target clients, clarify your branding and tailor your services.

- Use your client persona to define your referrer personas, who are the ideal people to introduce you to your target clients.

- Understand that your value proposition is the reason your clients choose you and can be thought of in the equation: value = benefits - costs.

- Send existing clients and referrers a survey asking why they choose you and note down the words and phrases that they use to help define your value proposition.

- Figure out what your value proposition is for your referral partners, which is the value you need to provide to them in order to gain access to their contacts. This is different to your value proposition for clients, as any value you provide to referral partners will only ever be a nice-to-have and not a service they will pay for.

- Offer something of value to both the ideal referrer and the ideal client that directly relates to your expertise and is free for both.

Referral metrics

- A successful referral strategy depends on data and accurate analysis of it through metrics. Experiment with what works and think of failure as data. Conduct tests, collect data and use it to generate further insights and ideas to test. Use failure to refine your referral strategy.

- The key metrics for a service business are the client lifetime value, conversion rate, cost of acquisition and churn rate.

- The client lifetime value for clients gained through referrals tends to be higher than for those obtained in any other way. CAC (the cost of acquiring each new client) is potentially huge for service businesses. It is only justified because the CLTV of clients is high.

- Identifying the conversion rate of your different marketing and business development efforts will help you put resources in the right place and identify blockages in your marketing funnels.

- A referred client should churn less than clients who come to you by other means. Reducing your churn rate will have the surest impact on your business's success.

- The best referrer is one who regularly introduces clients to you who have a high CLTV, high CR, low CAC and low churn rate. But given the lack of data, to make use of metrics in your referral strategy you will need to take a step back and think in terms of referrer personas rather than individual referrers.

- Track the effectiveness of your referrer personas over time. Key data are your average RP billings and your average RP referrals. If you notice that your best RPs are sending you fewer referrals than before, or the fees generated are lower, investigate urgently.

- Referral fees constitute a great additional income stream that involve little work on your part, but a referral fee should never be the reason for making an introduction. Only make referrals to service providers who you believe will do a great job.

Strategic relationships

- Service businesses rarely have enough data to make decision based purely on the numbers so you have to obtain qualitative data from conversations with your clients and referral partners. This is an opportunity for service businesses as your relationships are key, and the process of exploration and getting to know people is part of the relationship-building process.

- Your best referrers are likely to be your clients, your friends and your colleagues. Consider repeat work from the same client as a referral to stop you from taking your existing clients for granted.

- Once you have identified your best referrers, give them the red-carpet treatment. Take your clients and top referrers for drinks, dinners, coffees and any other form of informal contact that is appropriate for the relationship. Bond over shared interests like theatre and, if you must, golf.

- After a client project has completed, invite your client for dinner to say thank you for the work. Ask the client to invite four or five of their contacts who might also benefit from your services. Clients love doing this, because it allows them to add value to their contacts too. At the dinner, don't sell to them, but try to understand any problems they have. You're trying to find an excuse to keep in touch after the dinner.

- Treat your best referrers like human beings, not prospects or targets. Arrange to see them just because you want to spend time with them. Regularly ask your key referrers for help. Whether it's advice on their area of expertise or emotional support, asking for help is a great way to know, like and trust each other more.

- Give referrals to receive referrals. What goes around does seem, eventually, to come around.

- Add clients and your best referrers to your list for greetings for seasonal and religious festivals. Send out seasons' greetings for the main religious and cultural groups.

- Always say thank you for referrals. Send small gifts (at the relevant season or as a thank you for a referral) that are linked to your brand in some way. A little creativity goes a long way to help them remember you.

- At the end of each quarter or year, make a note of clients you think have churned or referrers who have stopped referring work and contact them. Ask for feedback and try to reconnect.

- For large enterprise clients, identify the internal referral opportunities. Which other departments should you be speaking to? Who makes the decisions?

- If a reliable referrer moves to a different business, keep in touch with them. By being thoughtful during a time of change for them, you will strengthen your personal bond and find yourself with an advocate in a new potential client business.

- Ask for referrals from your best referrers. Say, 'we have capacity to take on one more client at the moment. Who do you know that might benefit from talking to us?'

- The best referrers should become strategic partners in your business. Try hosting events together, approaching clients together and branding your work together.

Leverage marketing to drive referrals

- The role of marketing in your referral strategy is to reinforce your personal brand and the brand of your firm by making explicit who your clients are and what your value proposition is. Specifically, marketing must help clients and referral partners know, like and trust you.

- Most service businesses do not receive work directly from their marketing alone. Referrals are much more powerful for most service businesses than pay-per-click advertising or search engine optimisation.

- Your website is the foundation of your know, like and trust marketing. As you are targeting referral partners in your sector or profession, it does not just need to impress the uninformed, it needs to impress other experts too.

- The referrer or client already thinks you are good, that's why they have come to your website. They check you out online to verify that opinion, so your website needs to help them trust you. Don't give them a reason not to.

- When looking at your website, clients and referral partners should have no doubt that you are qualified to do the work they need you to do. Any doubt here makes receiving the referral less likely.

- A good personal profile photograph is entry-level like-and-trust marketing. Ensure the style of photograph is the same across your team to reinforce your credibility.

- If your business primarily grows by referrals, have a page on your website setting out the importance of referrals to you and how you roll out the red carpet for them. If you have a referral scheme set this out too, including exclusive contents, referral fees, discounts or free services for your referral partners.

- Write informative content and provide actionable information for newsletters and publication on your website and posting on social media. Content should focus on problems faced by clients rather than how great you are. Show, don't tell how you help solve their problems.

- Even if you are not focusing on using SEO to draw prospects to your website, consider asking an SEO expert to review your online written content to ensure it is easy to read and focused.

- Video of you talking to camera explaining how you will resolve a client's problem reminds people what you do. More than written content, it is a great way for clients and referral partners to gain a sense of who you are and whether they will like and trust you.

- Your referral partners will share your content more if they feature in it. Invite your referral partners to guest write a blog or interview them on a webinar or podcast.

- Create free content for use by your best referrers. Content creation is difficult, so they will be grateful for your insights if it is relevant to their clients and they can use it for their website or newsletter.

- Newsletters remind your referral partners and clients what you do. Include practical advice on solving problems and news on recent changes or upcoming deadlines. You'll be the first person they come to when they, or someone else, needs your services again.

- Find what social media platforms your referral partners tend to use and focus your attentions there. Content needs to be tailored to the medium on which you are using it. Interactions on social media can mimic interactions in a room full of referral partners so post on other peoples' posts and respond to requests for work.

- Case studies show clients and referrers that you have the necessary expertise, how you approach a problem, and what they can expect in terms of solution and timeframe. Not having testimonials rings alarm bells. Integrate review, testimonial and case study requests into your client onboarding and exit processes.

Networking

- Networking is the ground war of your referral strategy. Networking should be fun and efficient, as well as fun because it is efficient. Successfully making valuable friendships and lucrative referral partnerships is a great feeling. Measure the success of your networking efforts with the networking funnel.

- Attend online networking events including classes, webinars and virtual conferences. If the event is worth going to, concentrate on it throughout. After an online webinar, send a personalised message to each of the speakers and other selected attendees.

- Attend real world networking events such as industry conferences, trade shows, workshops, local business events and policy forums. Networking should be fun, because then you'll keep doing it. Put your humanity first, find the events you enjoy going to and only then start thinking about referrals.

- Your personality type informs what events you go to and also how you behave at those events. To leverage membership groups and networking events, build an efficient networking funnel and plan what to attend based on who you are, otherwise you will hate the process and it will not be sustainable.

- There are always more sellers than buyers at events, putting buyers in a position of considerable power, so attend events where your targets are the sellers at those events and you will always be in the right room.

- Your event preparation should consist of identifying your best categories of referrers, reviewing the list of attendees to see who in these categories is attending, deciding what value you will offer your referral partners and rehearsing your elevator pitch.

- Building rapport is key to gaining referrals and the best way to build rapport is to listen. In between listening, repeat your elevator pitch to everyone you meet to the extent that you are bored of saying it by the end of the event.

- Once you have found someone who meets your criteria of a good potential referral partner, start the relationship well by building up reciprocity debt by making useful introductions for them as soon as possible, ideally at the event itself.

- Explore different referral networks including chambers of commerce, local business clubs, sector-based groups, professional networks, groups based on personal characteristics like ethnicity or gender and government-sponsored networks.

- Create your own networking group. Assemble non-competing businesses that share your target audience to cross-promote each other's services and make referrals.

- Systematically follow up after you attend networking events and use tech to help you.

Scale referrals with technology

- Referrals are hard to scale because trust is hard to scale. Use technology to systematically grow your business through referrals. If you try to do this manually, you will soon stop focusing on referrals as a strategy. Technology does not just make your life easier: it allows you to know your clients and referral partners better, spot patterns and thrive.

- Before you invest in tech, review how you currently work, what data you currently collect and how it is stored. You may need an expert who understands customer relationship management and your referral strategy to conduct a review for you. Marketing and development experts will save you time, allowing you to focus on billable client work.

- The starting point of your referral tech is your CRM. It allows you to store your data in one place, identify your best referrers and communicate easily with them. Collect and use high-quality data to track performance of your referral strategy, monitor referrals, generate reports and make informed changes to your strategy.

- Based on the workflows you have devised for your business, create automations that periodically contact clients and referral partners with newsletters and bespoke emails, based on templates which draw in their data from your CRM.

- Prepare template emails by using those we have provided or asking AI to write the first draft. Save these templates in your email provider for easy access. Combine them with the data and automations in your CRM so that your emails will be personalised with the relevant names and other data.

- A referral strategy involves considerable face time with your referrers and clients. Use scheduling apps judiciously to reduce the time required to organise meetings. Integrate your video conferencing with an AI notetaker and record the information in your CRM.

- A data protection or cybersecurity breach will undermine even the best referral strategy and you have legal obligations to look after your contacts' data. Put and keep proper data protection protocols and cybersecurity in place. Use AI cautiously.

APPENDIX 2

THE STEPS PLAN

Project name: give the project a name.

Definitions: include the definitions you use in the steps plan.

Contacts: include the names, emails and phone numbers of all those involved as clients, advisers or third parties.

Key: colour code each step. For example: yet to start; drafts in circulation; agreed form; uploaded to e-signing; circulated for signing; documents signed; documents dated and action completed.

Document or Action	Deadline	Responsibility	Signatories	Notes
A. Research and Preliminaries				
1.				
2.				
3.				
4.				

Document or Action	Deadline	Responsibility	Signatories	Notes
B. Approvals				
1.				
2.				
3.				
4.				
C. Project section 1				
1.				
2.				
3.				
4.				
D. Project section 2				
1.				
2.				
3.				
4.				

Document or Action	Deadline	Responsibility	Signatories	Notes
E. Post Completion: Admin, Filings and Notifications				
1.				
2.				
3.				
4.				

You can find a landscape MS Word version of this document at: adviserly.io/working-with-strangers/

APPENDIX 3

TEMPLATE EMAILS

These templates are written in the author's personal style. We recommend amending them to suit your circumstances and align with professional and cultural expectations. Set them as templates in your customer relationship management tool or email provider, such as Microsoft Outlook.

These emails have been drafted with the assistance of artificial intelligence. We recommend using AI to assist in drafting your own bespoke templates too.

You can find a MS Word version of this document at adviserly.io/working-with-strangers/

Introducing one contact to another

Hi [name], I hope you are having a good week.

I'm very pleased to introduce you to [name] at [service provider], which provides [expertise] advice [among other things] in [jurisdiction].

No need to keep me copied in but please do let me know how it goes.

Best regards

Thanking a referrer for an introduction to a service provider and setting up a call

Hi [name], thank you so much for the introduction and hello, [name], it's great to meet you.

[Name], would you be free for a call in the next couple of [weeks] – always delighted to meet a recommendation from [name]. I'd love to hear more about your business, and explain a bit more about what we do at [organisation].

Let me know when suits, or if easier, please find a time that works for you using this [calendar link].

Best regards

Thanking a referrer for introducing a client and setting up a call

Hi [name], thank you so much for the introduction and hello, [name], it's great to meet you.

[Name], would you be free for a call in the next couple of [days] so I can understand more about your priorities, the work that needs doing, and explain a bit more about what we do at [organisation]. I will then be able to provide a quote for the work.

Let me know when suits, or if easier, please find a time that works for you using this [calendar link].

Best regards

Asking contacts for recommendations for particular services

Hi [name], I hope you are having a good week.

Would you be able to recommend a reliable [service provider] for a project for one of our clients. We are looking for someone who can assist with [description of the services needed].

Thank you in advance for your assistance.

I look forward to hearing from you soon.

Best regards

Asking contacts if they can do the work that needs doing

Hi [name], I hope you are having a good week.

Would you be able to assist on a project for one of our clients. We are looking for a [service provider] who can assist with [description of the services needed]. If so, would you be free in the next day or so? If convenient, please find a time that works for you on [calendar link].

Thank you in advance for your assistance.

I look forward to hearing from you soon.

Best regards

Asking clients or contacts for a catch-up call

Hi [name], I hope you are well. It's been a while since we last spoke.

Would you be free for a catch up soon? It would be great to find out how things are going and update you on [insert relevant recent changes or opportunities that relate to your expertise and their business].

When might work for you for a call? If more convenient, please use my [calendar link] to book a time that works for you.

Best regards

Follow-up after meeting someone at an event to set up a one to one

Hi [name], it was a pleasure meeting you at [event name] on [event date]. I enjoyed our conversation about [topic discussed].

We discussed the possibility of collaborating on [opportunity discussed].

When might work for you for a call to continue the conversation? If more convenient, please use my [calendar link] to book a time that works for you.

Looking forward to continuing our conversation.

Best regards

To a contact who misses an online meeting or call

Hi [name], I hope the day is going well. I think we had a call booked. Would you like to reschedule?

If convenient please book a time here [calendar link].

I look forward to speaking in due course.

Best regards

Reminders for any of these emails

Hi [name], I hope you are well.

Following up on my previous email, have you had the opportunity to consider [subject matter of the email]?

It would be great to carry on the conversation as there is [describe mutual benefit].

I look forward to hearing from you.

Best regards

APPENDIX 4

REFERRAL METRICS

The key metrics for your referral strategy are:

- Client lifetime value or CLTV (£) = the annual fees paid by a client x the number of years as a client.

- Conversion rate (%) = (number of new clients in a period / initial size of cohort in the period) x 100.

- Client acquisition costs or CAC (£) = total spend on acquiring new clients in a period / new clients in the period.

- Churn rate (%) = (the clients who leave you in a period / total number of clients in a period) x 100.

- Average referrals by referrer persona (#) = the number of paying clients received by referrals per category of RP / number of referrers in that category of RP.

- Average RP billings (£) = the fees billed by clients per category of RP that introduced them / number of referrers in that category of RP.

You can find a MS Excel version that automatically calculates your referral metrics at adviserly.io/working-with-strangers/

ABBREVIATIONS

AI   Artificial intelligence

API   Application programming interface

B2B   Business to business

BANT   Budget, authority, need, timeline

BTOP   Budget, team, other parties and planning

CAC   Client acquisition cost

CLTV   Client lifetime value

CRM   Customer relationship management

GDPR   General Data Protection Regulation

IFA   Independent financial advisor

IP	Intellectual property
PPC	Pay per click
RP	Referrer persona
SEO	Search engine optimisation
USP	Unique selling point

FURTHER READING

Edmund Burke, *Reflections on the Revolution in France*, London, 1790

Mark Carney, *Value(s): Building a Better World for All*, William Collins, 2021

Daniel Coyle, *The Culture Code, The Secrets of Highly Successful Groups*, Random House Business Books, 2018

Sean Ellis and Morgan Brown, *Hacking Growth: How today's fastest-growing companies drive break-out success*, Virgin Books, 2017

Malcolm Gladwell, *Talking to Strangers*, Allen Lane, 2019

Daniel Kahnemann, *Thinking Fast and Slow*, Farrar, Straus and Giroux, 2011

Erin Meyer, *The Culture Map: Breaking Through the Invisible Boundaries of Global Business*, Public Affairs, New York 2014

Kate Raworth, *Doughnut Economics: Seven ways to think like a 21st-century economist,* Penguin Books, 2017

Eric Ries, *The Lean Startup: How constant innovation creates radically successful businesses,* Crown Business, 2011

Steven Sinek, *Start with Why: How great leaders inspire everyone to take action,* Penguin Business, 2011

Matthew Syed, *Black Box Thinking: Why most people never learn from their mistakes but some do,* Portfolio, 2015

Chris Voss and Tahl Raz, *Never Split the Difference: Negotiating as if your life depended on it,* Random House Business, 2016

ACKNOWLEDGEMENTS

All books are team efforts; a book about working with strangers is even more so. Thank you first to you, dear reader, for bothering with the Acknowledgements, important but much underread.

In the collaboration between you as reader and me as writer, the real effort is yours. I hope to have sparked more ideas than just those which are contained in these pages.

Accountability is key to collaboration, so I own all mistakes, syllogistic or solipsistic, and ask your indulgence.

For all of the individuals and groups who have contributed ideas and comments on the themes, text and covers, the book is theirs too.

Ben Carew and Arnaud Mardegan's Othership community kept me, and many others, enthusiastic for work during and since the Covid lockdowns. It continues to show the power of collaboration between kind, generous and talented entrepreneurs.

The staff and coworkers at Soho Works in London kept me fuelled with coffee, pastries and entertaining conversation. They prove that a great venue can facilitate great referrals.

Analysis from Kirstin Lucas and Silke Jansen, hosts of the thePower's book club, helped me understand what business readers are looking for. The community of fellow students, overseen by the irrepressibly enthusiastic Molly Ronan, share an infectious love of learning and generosity of spirit that I have drawn on and tried to bottle.

I thank Joseph Gerstel and his Lawyerpreneurs, Christian Tooley's community of LGBT entrepreneurs at i3 investing and the 2016 cohort of global leaders from the International Visitor Leadership Programme for your time considering and selecting a great cover for this book.

For that design the thanks mainly goes to Chantel Barnett at Clear Design for conceiving and reworking many great concepts until we landed on an image that perfectly encapsulates what the book is about.

The community of legal service providers who took the time to comment on my interminable social media posts about collaboration helped hammer out the key themes. In particular, I am grateful to Kellie Simpson, Dan Warburton, Kirsty Pappin, Graham Wood, Clara Rose, Rachel Booth, Michael Hinchcliffe, Jason Adderley, Liz Smith, Jonathan Williams, Vanessa Ugatti, Jono Randell-Nash, Oliver Tromp, Lisa Summerton, Yvette Asker and Charlie Lawson.

The boutique law firms on the Adviserly network provided the inspiration and motivation. Their lessons and experiences run throughout the text. If we are going to build a world of empowered, collaborating communities, these firms are key to that success.

And then there are those entrepreneurs who provided wisdom I could not have thought up myself: Jules Zeng, Bill Cogan, Thad Cox, Alex Marinova, Kevin Smith, Kasvi Sehgal, Jimmy Vestbirk, Mike Adams, Will Timmins and Jack Lineker. The subjects of the case studies kindly allowed me to interview them to capture the real magic of how to grow a business through referrals. Chris Lee and Tim Coleman lent a fresh pair of eyes and made sure the text made sense.

Thank you to Rafael Gozalo, co-chief executive of thePower and prophet of innovation and learning, for his generous foreword to this book. I hope that the text delivers on the promise he identifies.

My publisher, Adam Jolly of Novaro Publishing, deserves special thanks for his efforts in honing the themes and text, making it readable and ensuring that some people actually buy it. I am particularly grateful for his early patience after a false start with another book proposal, entitled, appropriately enough, *Learning from Failure*.